How to Start a Legal Nurse Consulting Business

Book 1 in the "Creating a Successful LNC Practice" Series

Patricia W. Iyer, MSN RN LNCC

The Pat Iyer Group
Fort Myers, FL

Copyright

How to Start a Legal Nurse Consulting Business

Copyright 2016 Patricia Iyer. All rights reserved.

Cover design and layout by Douglas Williams

Editorial support by Constance Barrett

Published by:

The Pat Iyer Group
11205 Sparkleberry Drive
Fort Myers, FL 33913

No part of this publication may be produced or transmitted in any form or by any means, mechanical or electronic, including photocopying and recording, or by any information storage and retrieval system, without permission in writing from the editors, with the exception of reviewers, who may quote brief passages.

Disclaimer
The Publisher and Author make no representation or warranties with respect to the accuracy or completeness of this work and specifically disclaim all warranties, including without limitation warranties of fitness for a specific purpose. No warranty shall be created or extended by sales or promotional materials. The advice and strategies of the authors in this

work may not be suitable for all situations. This work is sold with the understanding that the Publisher is not engaged in rendering legal, accounting or other professional services. Neither the Publisher nor the Author shall be liable for damages arising herefrom.

The fact that an organization or website is referred to in this work as a citation or a potential source of further information does not mean that Author or Publisher endorse the information the organization or website may provide or recommendations it may make.

Further, readers should be aware that internet websites and email addresses listed in this work may have changed or disappeared between the time this work was written and when it is read.

This product contains affiliate links for products that Pat Iyer recommends for legal nurse consultants. She may receive compensation for her recommendations.

This product is for sale. To purchase a copy, and to collect your valuable free reports, go to: **www.legalnursebusiness.com.**

ISBN-13: 978-1523394012

About the Author

Patricia W. Iyer, MSN RN LNCC

President, The Pat Iyer Group,
Fort Myers, FL

www.legalnursebusiness.com

Patricia helps legal nurse consultants get more cases, make more money and avoid expensive mistakes through her coaching program, www.LNCAcademyinc.com. From 1989 to 2015, she was the President of Med League Support Services, Inc, which provides legal nurse consulting services to personal injury, malpractice, and product liability attorneys. She is a prolific author who has written, edited or coauthored over 675 articles, chapters, case studies, and online courses on a wide variety of nursing topics.

In the fall of 2008, Ms. Iyer launched a series of teleseminars for LNCs, now available on the www.legalnursebusiness.com website. Ms. Iyer is a well known and respected legal nurse consultant. She served for five years on the Board of Directors of the American Association of Legal Nurse Consultants, including a term as president. She was the chief editor of the Legal Nurse Consulting: Principles and Practices, Second Edition, the core curriculum for legal nurse consulting and Business Principles for Legal Nurse Consultants. She also served as the chief editor of the AALNC's online course. Ms. Iyer is certified as a legal nurse consultant by the American Association of Legal Nurse Consultants. AALNC awarded her with the Lifetime Achievement/Distinguished Service Award and with the Volunteer of the Year Award.

Reach Pat at patiyer@legalnursebusiness.com

Client Testimonials

"I have been a legal nurse consultant colleague of Pat Iyer's for almost 10 years. She is considered a leader among legal nurse consultants and has written multiple books on this subject which have offered guidance to us all. She is highly respected in her profession."

— KATHY G. FERRELL, BS, RN, LNCC

"Pat is an exceptional person who is highly dedicated and creative. She has excelled in many areas of health care and pioneered many aspects. It is a pleasure to be affiliated with Pat."

— KATHY MARTIN, LEGAL NURSE CONSULTANT

"Patricia is on one of the founders of legal nurse consulting. She has contributed substantially to the profession's growth as a leader in the field. I would highly recommend Patricia in this field."

— JANE BARONE, LEGAL NURSE CONSULTANT AND AUTHOR

"I worked with Patricia on a book project as one of her contributors and she was incredible. Professional and easy to work with — I don't know what else a person could ask for."

— DIANE WILEY, LEGAL NURSE CONSULTANT AND AUTHOR

" ... Great information and very comprehensive. If you need more information, please look at Pat Iyer's website and buy some of her programs. They will be well worth your money.

— KATHIE CONDON, LEGAL NURSE CONSULTANT

"Pat is a prolific author, extremely good. I have a shelf in my study bookcase area that is just hers. I learned a lot from her."

— PAT BEMIS, PAST PRESIDENT OF NATIONAL NURSES IN BUSINESS

"Pat's legal presentation at the Academy of Medical Surgical Nursing was thoughtful. It was engaging. It was interesting. It was well-thought out. I came away from that presentation with a lot of information I can take back to the staff where I work. We can tweak our practice and we can document in a more thoughtful manner. I would always go to a presentation that Pat was a part of.

—LINDA WILLETTE, RN

"I have had the pleasure and honor of meeting Pat Iyer. She is so professional. Just watching her has inspired me as a family nurse practitioner to be more professional. She has given workshops and speaking engagements. Everyone has attested to her knowledge in the field. She has written books. I wish that you too could take the opportunity to meet with her. She has a website. Take advantage of some of the materials she has to offer."

—LESLIE LEE, RN MSN

Contents

Copyright	iv
About the Author	vii
Client Testimonials	ix
Introduction: How to Start a Legal Nurse Consulting Business	xiii
Acknowledgments	xv
Chapter 1: Checking Your Mindset	1
Chapter 2: Avoiding Business Struggles	25
Chapter 3: Developing Your Business	53
Chapter 4: Getting Your First Case	67
Chapter 5: Creating Your Professional Image	99
Chapter 6: Attracting Your Prospects	119
Chapter 7: Reaching Out to Attorneys	147
Chapter 8: Asking for Referrals	161
Chapter 9: Managing Your Business	195
Chapter 10: Organizing Your Finances	227

How to Start a Legal Nurse Consulting Business

Introduction

Do you want to grow your business? Develop a group of raving fans who will recommend you to their colleagues? How do you build a strong business? One of the essential components of building a strong business is establishing a loyal customer base. This book is directed to legal nurse consultants to help them do just that. The principles here will help you to establish and maintain successful relationships with customers to build a solid business. There is an abundance of opportunity for legal nurse consultants. I will show how you to tap into it.

Running a business is a challenge for most entrepreneurs. Some legal nurse consultants may have to contact many potential customers to land a sale or contract. Well-established and respected legal nurse consultants may find they have more work than they can handle. Would you like to be in that situation? This book is geared to the consultant who is searching for tips to jump-start a consulting practice. Even after you make that first sale you have to be willing and able to follow the client through the client development process and move her from potential client or prospect to become a raving fan for you and your services.

In the years since I became a nurse, I have started five businesses. My nursing education taught me how to take care of patients but not how to run a successful business. In this book, I will share with you many lessons learned and best practices. The principles and tips in this book will help you gain success in your legal nurse consulting practice. At the end of most chapters, I have included books from my personal library that I have found to be valuable resources. Some of the links in this book are my affiliate links. I stand to gain financially if you sign up for the services I recommend and rely on myself.

I encourage you to read, explore, network, learn and grow!

Acknowledgments

The author appreciates the contributions of these individuals to the material in this book:

Karen Apy, RN LNCC

Kathleen Aston, BS, CEO of Kathleen Aston International, **www.kathleenastoninternational.blogspot.com**

Wendy Cassera, **www.taxpections.com**

Caryn Kopp, MBA, President of Kopp Consulting, **www.koppconsultingusa.com**

Debbie O'Grady, **www.theaccountabilitysquad.com**

Victoria Powell CCM, LNCC, CNLCP, MSCC, CEAS II, President of VP Medical Consulting, **www.vp-medical.com**

Lorette Pruden, PhD, **www.teamnimbusnj.com**

Jena Rodriquez, **www.brandwithjena.com**

Cheryl Schoen RN, **www.cisimages.com**

Therese Sparby, **www.theresesparby.com**

CHAPTER 1

Checking Your Mindset

Chapter 1

Checking Your Mindset

The idea of being self-employed motivates many nurses to take the step of investigating starting a business.

Some see legal nurse consulting as a part-time business; others intend to work their business full time. This book will help you, whether you want to start a business, keep your business part-time, or expand it into a successful, full-time business. If you are running a full-time business, this information will help you grow your business.

You don't decide to be an entrepreneur. Some say you get smacked on the head with an idea. Once you begin thinking like an entrepreneur, you learn to spot and evaluate opportunities. Only 5% of the population are entrepreneurs, but we create jobs for much of the rest of the population.

Negative Factors That Hold You Back

When I first thought of starting a business, I felt like I was stepping off a cliff. Would I fall and fail? Or would I soar? What is holding you back from starting your business or taking your business up a notch by expanding your services, staff, or overhead? Is it:

1. The economy?
2. The competition?
3. Your perception of your own inexperience?

There could be another explanation. What may be stopping you in your business is what you're telling yourself. It could be:

1. Lack of confidence
2. Limiting beliefs
3. Self-sabotage
4. Chronic procrastination
5. Lack of motivation
6. Fear of failure
7. Perfectionism

This chapter shows you how to overcome these limitations.

Qualities of Entrepreneurs

Who you are in life is who you are in business. Many entrepreneurs don't understand this. Whatever strengths and weaknesses you have are the personal traits you pack into your bag and take to your office. Once you arrive, you unpack them and put them on your desk.

What are you unpacking? Are you unpacking a positive mindset and positive self-talk? Are you unpacking great confidence and real, solidified, ultimate knowledge that you are skilled? Are you unpacking feelings of certainty and purpose, and courage to face obstacles and resistance? Are you unpacking solid principles to be able to self-validate your worth and success no matter what anybody else says?

Or is your bag loaded with fear, uncertainty, and doubt? Is it loaded with areas of diminished self-esteem? Is it loaded with a sabotaging mindset and negative self- talk? Is it loaded with feelings of inadequacy about certain of your abilities and is it loaded with a need for other people to approve of you so that you feel worthy and successful?

We all have a mixture of things in our bag. We have great things in our bag and we have not-so-great things in our bag. When we're entrepreneurs or when we're in business by ourselves, what's negative in that bag tends to be highlighted. Our weaknesses become more of a central focus and create more fear in us. We don't have that imagined safety net any more of working for a medical entity. Even though we watched the clinical layoffs over the last years, we sometimes forget that there's really no safety net at all. When we work for others, we feel a false sense of safety. We do not want to acknowledge that a JOB is the Journey of the Broke.

When we are self-employed, we have to acknowledge that we need to create our own safety net. If you read Stephen Covey's *7 Habits of Highly Successful People* or the works of many other noted gurus, you will learn that there are key differentiators between those in business who really take off and those who don't.

Successful entrepreneurs tend to have:
- A positive mindset

- A defined and sturdy concept of self, which includes self-esteem, self-confidence and other aspects of worthiness;
- High-achiever behaviors vs. perfectionist behaviors;
- Resilient characters.

If the road we're taking is not successful, we need to know it's not because we're not worthy or we're not good enough, it's that this wasn't the right road, so we need to take another road. Self-employed business people also need an ability to validate ourselves and not be dependent on external forces in the world. Don't rely on the positive or negative messages we get from other people to tell influence our feelings of worth.

Entrepreneurs spend a lot of time and money buying sales and marketing tools, sometimes at the expense of not really working on ourselves. We get caught up in the bright shiny object syndrome by buying the next course, the next book, or watching the next seminar. I have made this mistake myself. I like to buy marketing books. But just because I have marketing books on my bookshelf does not mean I have absorbed the knowledge through osmosis. I have to read them, underline them, and think about them to absorb the information. Another trap is that we end up with the cadre of business tools that are not working the way we hoped they would because we don't have our foundations of self confidence to use them to their full potential.

Fears

Fear holds many legal nurse consultants back. You've got to find something to help you get over this emotion. Let's examine what this fear means. The ability to fight it is the underpinning to building a positive mindset, the self-esteem and the confidence that you need to be truly successful. Fear will paralyze us and make it impossible for us to take action because we do not know where to head. So we need to stop and uncover what it is that we're afraid of; we also need to go back and find out where that fear originated and learn how to subdue it.

We develop these thought and belief patterns when we are very young. If we're told as youngsters that we're brilliant, smart, or funny, that message becomes our belief about ourselves. We're going to act out in ways that support our belief. We're going to act funny; we're going to act smart; we're going to act special; we're going to act as if we are attractive, whatever we've been told.

If we've been taught the opposite of that, we're going to act out that way. If you are told you have nothing important to say, you're going to turn that into a belief and you're going to act that way. This is not a conscious process. It's totally unconscious, but that is what happens.

It really comes down to self-worth. Ask yourself, "Why am I afraid? What am I afraid of? What happened in my past that has validated this *is* something to be afraid of, and what can I do to get out of the state of fear so that I can take my business/career to the next level?"

1. Have you received messages from family, friends, or foes that eroded your self esteem? Were you bullied? Abused? Put down?
2. Are you afraid of a business failure? Are you afraid of the embarrassment of having to admit that you failed?
3. Are you afraid that you're not good enough to help attorneys, no matter what your education?

In a survey I did of legal nurse consultants, half of the people said they were most afraid of not having enough revenue. The other half identified their chief fear as "feelings of inadequacy."

Fear is really a thought that's become a belief we have about ourselves that's revealed by the actions we take. We may fear that we won't get enough clients and that we'll go out of business or that someone won't like us or that we won't be good at our analysis of cases. When we think and dwell on that fear, we start to believe it to be true, and we sabotage ourselves through certain behaviors and actions that actually make those fears become our reality.

Quelling Fears

How comfortable are you with risk? In business there are no guarantees. There's no way to eliminate all the risk. You can improve; you can plan; you can prepare. You can do all those things, but you've got to know if you've got the passion to do it. You can be paralyzed by fears and lose your passion.

But thoughts and fears can be changed, and they can be replaced by more powerful thoughts. Once we come to grips with our fear, the panic starts to quiet, and we can start to hear our own inner self. We can strengthen our foundations of self to be successful in our life and in our business.

Let's take our fear of not enough revenue, which really comes down to us going bankrupt, being out of business, being financially destitute, or losing our home. What do you need to do tomorrow to start to ensure that your fear does not come true? Let's say that's your fear, and you do nothing. If you stay inactive and feel paralyzed and your mind just keeps spinning, you're going to become unfocused. You can't get out of it; the chances of that actually becoming reality for you have a much higher percentage.

I watched a friend of mine, a self-employed legal nurse consultant, literally go bankrupt. Her business dropped after changes occurred in the legal climate in her state. She was fearful of making changes and fearful of marketing. She seemed to have a fantasy that all would be well. She was not doing what she needed to hold onto her business, and she lost everything — her house, her business, and her bank account.

What she did *not* do was devise an action plan.

What are the steps you can take to keep the fear at bay? How do you push the fear away? For example, if you're afraid of not having enough money, there are several immediate things you can do:

1. You can reduce your expenditures. That is one of the easiest ways.
2. As soon as you're done with that, you need to look at your current client base and look at where you can up-sell them into additional services. Up-selling an existing client is easier than getting a new client.
3. The third thing you need to do is to immediately step up your marketing. Make cold calls, cold visits, and contact all of your clients. Ask for work.
4. You can also look for alternative sources of revenue. Can you work clinically a shift or two per week?

When you're stuck in fear, all your mental, physical, and emotional energy is focused on the fear. You're feeding it. The minute you take action, even if the first step is cutting expenses, you shift your focus. When you feed the fear, you draw it near. The minute you shift your focus, your mind stops feeding the fear, and that starts to push it away.

One of the techniques of neurolinguistic programming, or NLP, is to take a concept you fear and imagine it on a stage. You think about that fear and deliberately make it small. You push it further and further away until it is so tiny you can barely recognize it. I used this technique when I was experiencing great conflict with a business partner. I made him tiny, in my mind, and mentally pushed him away so that he did not overwhelm me.

By taking action you start to feel more in control. You start to feel less fearful because now you're controlling your business and marketing. Also you have more opportunities; as long as you have more opportunities you feel more optimistic. You've cut your expenses; you've called your accountant. Finding every actionable response to fear is the way to take the energy and put it into action and success.

The good news here is that fear is a thought and self-esteem is a thought. Thoughts can be changed. Thoughts are like programming in a computer. What we need to do is write a new program to override the old program. We need to take the negative thoughts, and we need to write a new program that has positive thoughts. At the end of this chapter, I'll talk about affirmations and their role in programming your thinking.

Mastering Mindset and Self-Esteem

Mindset and self-esteem are thoughts that determine how we think of ourselves, that show the world how we think through our behaviors and our actions. Most people identify themselves as having diminished self-esteem in some area of their life. Some people are great at business; they have total confidence in their business life, maybe not so much in their dating life. Some people are totally confident in their personal life and relationships as parents and friends and members of community, but don't have that confidence in their business life or perhaps in their social life. No one has 100% confidence.

We need to identify where the beliefs about ourselves come from. Then we need, as adults, to ask ourselves, "Is that really true about me? Am I not so smart? Am I not so brilliant? Or am I brilliant?" What's true now? What do you know intellectually to be true about yourself?

Here's an example. Let's say your father told you that you would be a great nurse and should stay away from business; you did not have a head for business. You went to nursing school thinking you'd be a great bedside nurse. You graduated and you shied away from management positions. After all, your father told you that you would not be good in business, and nursing management had a lot to do with budgeting, positions, product line and profits.

The next step of your process was learning about legal nurse consulting. You were attracted to the analytical, detail-oriented aspects of this field. You realized that few nurses were hired as employees of law firms, and that becoming self-employed was a common option. You realized you would need to parlay your clinical knowledge to start a business. You then realized you needed to reprogram negative thought patterns and overwrite them with a positive thought pattern, recognizing your strengths. You questioned your father's conclusions and looked at the reality of what you did well.

The goal is to leverage those strengths, those foundations that are already strong and then work on growing the confidence in the areas that are a little shaky. Some legal nurse consultants have a little bit of work to do; others have a lot of work to do to improve self-esteem.

Self-confidence is the muscle that's built when you have the self-esteem to take action repeatedly until a skill is mastered. It's very much like being a golf player. You need to learn how to play the game. You need to first learn how to hold the club, and you practice and practice; you build the muscles necessary to play the game. But before you go out to the golf course, you have to have a belief inside yourself somewhere, even if it's at an infinitesimal level, that you can actually play golf.

Because if you didn't have that belief inside yourself somewhere at some level, no matter how small, you'd never walk out to the course.

Your self-esteem as a legal nurse consultant has to be rooted in beliefs that you can succeed. It may need to be really bolstered and brought out, practiced and solidified. Self-confidence is born out of our belief that we can accomplish something. We build our muscle by practice over and over and over and over again until we master that skill.

I remember how I felt the first time I exhibited at a conference for attorneys. I had spent a lot of money to get my booth ready, to register for a table, and to assemble my materials. I lacked confidence in my skills.

I remember wanting to hide behind the booth — afraid someone would talk to me and find out I was inexperienced, and afraid no one would talk to me and I would have spent the money in vain. The irony was that I met an attorney at that conference who realized how I could help him and gave me so much work that my income from his business put my oldest son through an Ivy League college.

Mindset and self-esteem are very close — you really are what you think, consciously and unconsciously. Buddha said: "We are what we think, all that arises, with our thoughts we make the world." If you believe that you are special, that you are worthy, that you are capable, that you are deserving, that's what you will attract. If you believe that you are unworthy, you are not capable, you are not knowledgeable, that will shine through in your behavior and in your nervousness, and that's what you will become. We become what we think.

Self-esteem is your opinion of yourself and your opinion about how other people view you or think of you. We need to raise our level of self-esteem by reprogramming our thoughts with positive thoughts and affirmations.

Remember the children's book, *The Little Engine That Could*? This was a story about an engine that lacked self-confidence. He told himself, "I think I can, I think I can" as he climbed up a steep mountain. He was exultant on the other side, and steamed away, saying, "I knew I could, I knew I could." My oldest son loved that book!

If we don't turn our thoughts from "I *think* I can" to "I *know* I can," we start to slide back down that personal or business mountain we are climbing. Even when we look down, we need the mindset that doesn't say, "I'm going to fall." Instead, we say, "Wow. I've made it a long way up! I'm doing really well; look how far I got!"

That's what happens to us in business. We have to practice that and reprogram our thoughts and self-esteem no matter what happens and what the outcome. That's what we need to do as successful business owners. No matter what the outcome, you do not stop.

Each time after the first time I exhibited at an attorney conference, it got easier to stand in front of my table and greet strangers. Before I got into legal nurse consulting, I went through some training to be part of a multi-level marketing company and one of the things that we were told was that you do not fail, you simply achieve unintended outcomes. I also learned to deal with rejection, and to realize that every person who said "no" to my business opportunity brought me closer to the person who would say, "yes"!

Building Confidence

A confident business owner cannot be rattled by a negative outcome or an outcome that was less than favorable or by other people's criticism.

Limit or, if possible, eliminate negative people from your life. These are people who will say, "You know, you're crazy to try this, you'll never succeed." The term for those people is "dream stealers." They should be avoided because they'll step on your enthusiasm and make you stop before you can even start. Negative people are one of the biggest destructive forces to entrepreneurs. Entrepreneurs are such a different breed. We have big dreams; we take more risks; we want to do something big; we want to step out. A lot of people don't ever do that.

Be aware of the risks of listening to all this negative talk. All business owners make mistakes and achieve unintended outcomes. You *are* going to fall. You're going to take wrong turns; that's part of the journey. But if we're listening to all this negative talk, the first time we fall down we'll think, "Maybe they're right, maybe I can't do that." Do you see how that starts our own fear process going? And how they can erode confidence?

Entrepreneurs understand the mindset of another entrepreneur wanting to do something big, of taking that risk to achieve this big goal, of doing something big and amazing in this world. We need to be surrounded by other entrepreneurs.

Goal Setting

There are many ways that people develop self-confidence. The best way to build confidence is when you're backed by a plan. This way you can get to exactly where you're trying to go. You're reliant on each baby step that you take. Set goals. We understand how to set goals for patients. Do we apply the same process to our business?

A goal is very specific; you can measure it. You may set up a graph and keep track of your results. What can you measure? Here are just a few items:

1. Make 20 marketing calls each week
2. Send out 25 mailings each week
3. Gain 3 new clients per month

4. Convert 75% of potential cases into actual cases
5. Send out 100 invoices this year
6. Reduce invoices that are 30 days past due by 50%
7. Spend no more than 5 hours to locate an expert witness

Goals should be attainable. Many times we set goals that are unrealistic and not attainable. That sets us up for failure and is another way to totally diminish our confidence and self-esteem. We need to make sure that they're attainable and that the time that we're allowing ourselves is realistic. Goals should be specific. We should be able to define what we expect to achieve.

Be as specific with your goal writing as possible. You might want to say something like "I feel incredibly empowered, encouraged, and optimistic knowing that I have completed 20 sales calls every week for the last 90 days that have resulted in 45 new conversations and 18 new clients."

That's your goal, but you're writing it as if it's already happened. Do you see how specific it is? It's specific about the timeframe and about the quantity of calls. You could even add a revenue number into that goal because where the mind focuses, the mind goes.

Think of goals as short-term and long-term, a model we understand from nursing. Short-term goals break the big goal into tiny steps so we don't get overwhelmed with the big goal. We get encouraged and gain momentum by achieving the small goals. Every step brings you closer to the big goal, when you start to experience that feeling of personal and financial freedom, of fearlessness, of being empowered, of knowing who you are, of having strength and choice in your life as well as control of your life. Set your goals high so they stretch you, but realistically, so that you can grow and enjoy the accomplishment.

Set quarterly goals. Break them into steps with specific deadlines. Then review your quarterly goals at least every other week, adjust deadlines, and highlight those that are accomplished. Enjoy the process of accomplishing your goals. Use your quarterly goals to energize and focus you to appreciate what you have accomplished. You'll read more about goal setting in Chapter 9.

Creating Focus

Reduce interruptions to greatly improve your productivity. Why do we allow interruptions? A lot of times our fears, chaos, lack of direction, and inability to draw healthy boundaries mean we allow a lot of interruptions. They may come in the form of our phone, email, social media, or people walking in and out of the room. We can't get anything done. So at the end of the day we're frustrated and annoyed, which again diminishes our confidence and our self-esteem. We need to be in charge of our boundaries and our time.

Protect your environment by eliminating things that make you feel overwhelmed, unproductive, anxious, unhappy, and exhausted. Keep a clean, uncluttered desk. Put away papers you do not need to refer to and that only serve to distract you. Limit how often you check email.

As entrepreneurs we need to protect our energy, our time, and our mindset. Those are the three things we need to protect at all costs because everything is reliant on our abilities and how we feel when we work.

Self-Sabotage

Self-sabotage evolves from fear. The four key ways this shows up in our businesses are

1. chronic procrastination,
2. addiction to perfection,
3. lack of motivation and action, and
4. obsessive comparison to others.

Self-sabotage is driven by fear — fear of failure, fear of success, or fear of ridicule. If you don't try, you can't fail, right? If you don't fail, you can still maintain this flimsy belief: "I didn't fail." You haven't tried.

If you're never in a position to fail you can maintain that you're still good enough. You think, "If I do fail, then everything I fear is true. There's no way I can embarrass myself if I don't try and no one will be able to judge me."

Effects of Self-Sabotage

There are a lot of people who cannot follow through because self-sabotage gets in the way. You can overcome these things. You can practice handling fear of rejection by taking action, building self-esteem by going back to the origins of thoughts and reprogramming a positive mindset over a negative one.

In Chapter 4, I discuss making cold calls and cold visits to attorneys. Some of these contacts are going to result in rejection. Some of the law firms already use legal nurse consultants and do not want to switch to your services. Some of the firms will have employees who are trained to not put through any sales calls. You will be rejected. Expect it, and let it roll off your back.

All self-sabotage is harmful. It's unconscious behavior. A lot of times we don't realize that we're doing it or we don't realize why we're doing it. It stifles our business activities and revenues because of chronic financial stress. We get anxious over not getting something done or doing something at the very last minute. Even though you know intellectually that you need to get it done, you can't seem to get out of your own way. That feeds your lack of self-worth, low confidence and low self-esteem. You can't achieve anything in that state of being.

Procrastination and Perfectionism

There is also something called the *perfect procrastinator*. This links the perfectionist and the procrastinator. The perfectionist has to do things over and over and over again. The end product is never good enough, and therefore it never sees the light of day. Or, the perfectionist completes the report for the attorney, but bills the attorney for an unreasonable amount of hours. The attorney is pleased with the work product but horrified by the bill.

There's an extreme difference between striving for excellence and striving for perfection. Excellence is achievable; perfection is not. In striving for perfection, all we can do is fail and alienate our clients. In striving for excellence, we make lots of forward movement; we gain ground and we take an analytical look at what we can do better next time. It's a growth process.

Perfectionism and procrastination become very tightly linked. We all procrastinate to some degree but it is chronic procrastination that is most harmful.

I saw this in myself when I first launched my business. I knew I needed a work product sample. I decided to create a sample work product on the liability issue of delay in diagnosis of appendicitis. I must have spent 40 hours working up this sample. I did a literature review, a chronology, and an analysis of liability. I put it together in a binder and indexed and tabbed it. Then after reaching the end of the project, which had allowed me to procrastinate about marketing my services, I finally sent it out to an LNC to get feedback. I later realized that I had spent way too much time perfecting and procrastinating, and no one really cared about my sample report as much as I did. When I called her to ask her opinion of my sample, she had not even read it.

Do you know a nurse who says she is going to become a legal nurse consultant? She says, "I'm going to do this." She's so enthusiastic; she's so upbeat; she's really very persuasive because she's usually quite intelligent.

Six months later you meet her and you ask, "How is your business?" She says, "Oh you know, I got into it and it turned out it just wasn't that great an idea…but I've got this other idea, this is what I'm doing now."

You see her six months later and you ask, "So how did that new idea turn out?" She says, "You know, I got half-way through and it just wasn't a good idea."

Do you want to be a non-starter? Do you want to get stalled in the growth of your company? Do you strive to become perfect and procrastinate while you watch your competitors take on your potential clients?

Overcoming Procrastination

Here are three steps for overcoming procrastination that you can take right away. Some of these may seem simple, but many people don't do them. If you commit to doing these, you will find yourself making progress. This will improve your self esteem and your confidence.

1. *Create a cone of silence.* On your calendar you need to select a particular day or four hours when you're going to disconnect from everything. Work on one of your important initiatives. Continue to do that until that initiative is finished. Hopefully, you can take that initiative and know all the steps you need to take; plan out the hours. Do not answer your phone. Close down your social media. Don't take interruptions. Put a sign on the door of your office to let everybody know, "Do not disturb me."

The only person you need to fight is your inner procrastinator or the person who wants to wander away, who can't get focused. Direct yourself during these few hours to do these particular tasks. Don't move from that spot until those particular tasks are done.

You need to make a commitment to yourself because when you fulfill that commitment to yourself, you're going to feel so good, and the next time you go back it's going to be a little bit easier. Then you'll find yourself thinking about something you would rather do. Stop yourself; you want to go to that next level, and every time you do that, it feeds the muscle. Shut out the world and the noise of the world, which is overwhelming these days, to get your task done, build your confidence and keep the fear away.

2. *Make sure you are working on your unique talents.* Every one of us has unique talents, but what we find as entrepreneurs is that we end up doing all these other things. They're not our top unique talents. There are things that you or I do better than anyone else. I once heard an internet marketer freely admit he was good at creating products and lousy at all other things. I thought, "Isn't it amazing that he can so candidly admit his strengths and weaknesses?" After being raised to never admit to a weakness, I had to unlearn this behavior.

When we do things that we're good at, that have a lower failure rate attached to them, or that we're not personally invested in, we protect our talent and our feelings. We spend our time doing things we're good at. We're spending our time getting self-validated that we're good at something.

3. *Delegate things you do not like doing and that you are not good at.* For me it's QuickBooks and financial management. I am not good with numbers. I delegate that function to others who are much better at that work. You need to look at where you're spending your time and stop doing things that you're not good at, that are energy drains and a total waste of your time. Outsource them, delegate them, or don't do them. You need to make sure that 70-80% of your time as a business owner is spent working in your areas of talent and in nothing else.

Create your cone of silence, identify your talents, and don't take on anything else. Don't indulge in the self- sabotaging behavior of overloading yourself if you fail. That's a perfectionist behavior. You need to commit to yourself that you're not going to take on anything that isn't absolutely necessary for you to do until you get your initiative done. You need to honor your commitments to yourself.

Affirmations

Many people develop affirmations, or positive self-talk, to overcome self-confidence and self-esteem issues. Your affirmation might be that you want to have 100 clients within 2 years. I remember buying a filing cabinet many years ago and saying that I wanted to fill it up with case files. You need to say affirmations a lot because you're reprogramming your thinking.

Repeating your affirmations over and over and over again makes them become ever more deeply ingrained and grooved into your mind and your unconscious. After a while the new thought pattern takes over for the old thought pattern.

Say your affirmations aloud in the car. These things become your new thoughts; they become your new defaults.

Look at your procrastinations. What holds you back from making marketing calls, working on cases, or sending out invoices? Do you struggle with making collection calls? See where you're procrastinating. What are your fears? Why are you procrastinating? What's the fear that's keeping you from moving forward? Is that fear a reality? Is that something that's really going to happen or just a fear of impending doom?

Take time to go back and remember what it feels like to accomplish something of note. Remember that feeling of satisfaction when you really did something, when you finished it and it came out well. Think of how good it made you feel. Get back in touch with that feeling of positive emotion, outcome, and energy, and of actually completing the task. Define how to move forward with what you're procrastinating about.

You may never totally conquer your fears, perfectionism or procrastination, but you can use the techniques in this chapter to recognize the issue. Think about the impact on your career as a legal nurse consultant.

Tackle the issues. Set achievable goals and use affirmations to influence your mindset. Strive for a positive way of looking at the world and avoid negative thinking and people. The entrepreneurial spirit is a special one. Treasure the fact that you have the courage to set your course as you embrace the challenges of this interesting field of nursing. Consider and positively manage how your mindset affects the way you tackle the challenges of starting and running a business.

CHAPTER 2

Avoiding Business Struggles

CHAPTER 2

Avoiding Business Struggles

Chapter 1 addressed some of the critical issues that may interfere with our ability to build a thriving business: self-esteem, fear, procrastination, and other issues. This chapter goes deeper into solutions for building your business without struggle or suffering.

We struggle and suffer when we believe that our work needs to be difficult, when we take on burdens out of a false sense of responsibility, and deny ourselves time for pure enjoyment. Would you want to hire a consultant who looked as if she were carrying the burdens of the world? Neither do your potential clients.

Suffering can also occur when you don't know how to establish rapport. Your attorney client wants to feel a connection to you, a sense of comradeship, and the trust that you will serve his or her best interests.

Another big issue emerges in the form of difficult clients and power struggles. *Games People Play* by Eric Berne, M.D. was a very popular book in the 1970s because it taught people how to understand the mental and emotional games that impacted their lives. People are still playing games, and if you are a habitual victim, you will not do well in negotiations with a villain. You will learn more about victims and villains later in the chapter.

I have had to deal with all of the above issues. Mastery is key to the success of your legal nurse consulting business—or any business.

The Questions Beneath the Questions

You might think that your questions about building a business are: "How do I make more money?" or "How do I make running my business easier?"

These questions, though, may represent only the tip of the iceberg. Below are what might be some of your deeper questions.

- "How do I get more clients so that I can be happy?"
- "How do I make more money so that I can be happy?"
- "How do I stop working so hard in my business so that I can be happy?"

This dynamic implies suggests that your business has to provide the happiness and joy that you desire. Let's try looking at this from the opposite perspective: that *attitude* is primary. You have within you the potential to create unlimited happiness and joy.

Remember the section in Chapter 1 about affirmations? See what happens if you create and regularly state an affirmation such as: "My life provides me with all the happiness and joy I could ever desire" or whatever variation best suits you. If the belief that your happiness comes from within is the ground on which you stand, you'll find that getting more clients, earning more money, achieving the next level of success in your business, or feeling fulfilled comes naturally.

It will come without your having to work hard. If you strongly believe that you have to work very hard to make it in life, and you think less of people who are having fun and having easy lives, examine these beliefs. They are actually preventing you from having the success you want.

Return to affirmation mode with something like, "I love the work I do, and I do it with ease." That will give you a start, and this chapter will take you further. We'll explore the roots of why you may feel overwhelmed and worn out and what to do about it.

I'm going to give an example of someone who lives a happy life. It may sound strange to some of you because my example is a cat.

Anyone who has a cat in their lives can tell you that cats don't do anything that isn't easy or fun. I've learned from my cats that if it isn't easy and fun, something is wrong either with what I'm doing or with how I'm going about it.

Now I'm going to share the first ingredient for success.

How to Attract Clients with Ease

You've come into contact with potential clients through your website or through a referral. You want them to walk away with one thought in their minds: "I want what she's having."

If you're comfortable with the idea that you live a happy life in which work is easy, this will reflect in your interactions with potential clients. They'll feel some of what you're feeling, and they'll want more. They'll want to hire you.

Affirmations, as I said before, are the first step. Some other distinctions also come into play.

Awareness

The first one is "Awareness and Responsibility." What does that mean?

Awareness means both deepening and sharpening your focus and looking at levels that you've never explored before. It means learning to be a detective, studying everything and looking for clues. This looking is without judgment or the intention to fix anything. It is the simple and pure act of observation.

- "What's running well?"
- "What am I getting?"
- "Am I getting what I want?"

In this state, there is no need for reaction. You are trying to solve a puzzle with an open and clear mind.

As a legal nurse consultant, you already have this ability. A lot of what we do is to be very analytical, to pick apart a case, and to look at medical records to find the one or two words in that medical record that changes the whole complexion of the case.

Analysis and assessment skills are foundations for legal nurse consulting and in fact for being a nurse. We're all trained in how to collect data and then look at the data and formulate a plan and carry it out and then see if it worked. That's the heart of nursing, so analysis and responsibility fall naturally into the realm of what nurses and legal nurse consultants do as part of their role.

The caveat here is that what comes so naturally and logically to a nurse or legal nurse consultant may not seem so natural in your personal life or in running your business. In analyzing these areas, you may have to make a conscious effort to leave out the judgment. Remind yourself to adopt a professional attitude. Don't think of how you run your life or business as wrong or, worse, condemn yourself for any mistakes. You need only to analyze the facts.

To take it a step further, don't think about what you can change. The word change implies that something is broken. Something needs to be healed. Return always to the concept that you are fine. You don't need to fix anything. You are perfect as you are. What we do here is to replace the word "change" with "transformation."

Transformation

Stop here for a moment to take this in. I realize that transformation is a radical concept. Einstein said that we can't solve a problem at the level where we created it. This means we have to come up with creative and radical solutions. Transformation takes our thinking and our power to an entirely new level.

People respond to this concept in interesting ways. Some feel relieved and happy. Others are blown away. Some insist they aren't perfect, and they can never believe that they are. Still more say that they now feel committed to overcoming the fear of failure.

The concept of perfection is especially challenging. Perfect doesn't mean no room for transformation. It means that you begin with the idea that you are whole and ready to grow, that judgment doesn't belong in how you look at yourself.

Responsibility

This word is often misunderstood. Too often it has overtones of guilt, as in "Take responsibility for your mistakes." To me, it means "To be able to respond, response able."

The word "power" in French is translated as "to be able." Awareness shows us a new and deepened way of seeing what needs to be done. Responsibility gives us the ability to turn awareness into new action. Together, they keep us from running on the default setting.

This is very important for any entrepreneur. Have you ever felt like you're just running on autopilot, or doing the next thing that needs to be done, or not even knowing how you drove to work in the morning? We are creatures of habit, and habit is safe and comfortable. It's all too easy to get stuck in the rut of default.

So often, though, especially when we are entrepreneurs who need fresh and creative thinking to grow our business, our defaults no longer serve us. Stop, pull those up to the light of awareness, and notice whether or not they're working, and then choose. You may say, "This one is still working for me, so I'll continue with it." Or you may say, "This thought is no longer serving me, so I'm no longer going to choose that course of action."

What matters is having the freedom to make the choice.

If your business or life are not where you want them to be, when you turn up the magnifying glass on awareness, you can simply choose something different. This gives you the power so that circumstances are no longer to blame for anything that's happening in your life or business. You get to take the "Power Ball" back.

Overwhelm

We can use the concepts of awareness and responsibility to look at the problem of overwhelm. We'll explore its origins, how it operates, how it impacts your life and business, and then to remove it from our operating field so that we can meet powerful people on an even playing field and how to land contracts with ease.

I'm going to use an elephant to explain the importance of different perspectives. We'll look at different slices or pieces of the elephant from different angles.

If you had never seen an elephant before and, with your eyes closed, touched the trunk or the tail, you would have an incomplete and possibly entirely inaccurate image of it. The tools I'm going to use to describe different perspectives may also seem incomplete, but they are all going to come together in a complete picture.

I'll remind you again that we aren't working with the concept of change but that of transformation. I will show you how transformation does not have to take a long time or be hard. It builds through one choice at a time.

How Do We Get Overwhelmed?

The first elephant angle we're going to take a look at is the trunk.

What is it that causes overwhelm? You may be a full-time nurse but also trying to build a legal nurse consulting business. For the latter, you need to try to create leads, follow up on them, do other forms of marketing, and much more. Attorneys may ask for work samples that you don't have or make other requests. You're trying to juggle multiple aspects of your work life, and this doesn't even take into account the fact that you have a family or private life, too.

You want to look cool and collected, calm and happy, but you don't feel that way. You're struggling; life feels unbalanced; you worry about your family. You honestly come by your anxiety and overwhelmed feelings.

It doesn't have to be this way. Take a moment and think of things you say yes to in your business that are contributing to your feelings of being overwhelmed.

When I've asked legal nurse consultants about what overwhelms them, I've gotten a variety of answers. One was, "Going through a case with massive amounts of medical records."

Remember my comments about perception. An attorney called me once and said, "Oh, the medical records are voluminous. There are 750 pages." I was sitting there looking at a case in my office that had 17 three-inch binders of medical records. So we discovered that massive amounts of medical records are really in the eye of the beholder, i.e., subjective.

Other nurses have commented on the difficulty of maintaining the balance between an active clinical practice and a part-time business. Some say they feel overwhelmed by work that isn't interesting, and still more are overwhelmed by the attempt to fix problems fairly and quickly.

"Yes" and "No"

Here are two questions to ask about any situation that's making you feel overwhelmed. "Why do you say yes to these things? What is the payoff?"

Don't be fooled by the deceptive simplicity of this answer. If you can employ this in your life and in your business, you will reap ridiculous rewards.

The cure for overwhelm is clear "YESes" and clear "NOs." If you say yes to something or you allow something into your life, i.e., choosing to volunteer, working with a certain attorney, agreeing to reduce your fees, is your yes clear?

Clear "NOs" include, "No, I will not reduce my fees because I know that I feel taken advantage of and I get frustrated." "No, I can't take on an additional shift."

Clear "YESes" and clear "NOs" allow others to know how to be in relationship to you in a way that serves everyone.

Have you ever heard the line, "Good fences make good neighbors?" It usually gets misused in a way that justifies putting up barriers that cut off relationships and connections. The real meaning of this phrase is to set boundaries with clear

"YESes" and clear "NOs." If people don't know your boundaries, you're setting up both them and yourself for frustration.

You train people how to be in relationship to you somewhat in the manner you train a puppy. When you bring a puppy home for the first time, it needs to know where it can and cannot go to the bathroom. If the puppy is allowed to just run around, pee on the rug all over the place, and pee on chairs and couches and everything it will never learn how to be potty trained.

Clear boundaries enable that dog to understand that "When I have to go to the bathroom, I go to the door." In the same manner, you need to train people about your "YESes" and "NOs." If you don't, they will continue to pee all over the carpet, and they will cross the lines in your boundaries all the time. It will become more and more frustrating to you. What transforms your understanding is the realization that you trained them to treat you this way.

The good news is that you can retrain them. If there are relationships where you haven't set up your boundaries well, determine how you want to set them, recommit to them for yourself, and communicate them to the other person. Boundaries cannot be murky or confusing. They have got to be very clear, i.e., "No, not on the couch. Outside is okay."

The primary rule combating overwhelm is that if it's not a clear "YES", it's a "NO." If you don't get really excited about an opportunity, for example, working with an attorney on a specific project or getting paid a certain amount, that means it's not a clear "YES." It's a "NO."

In saying no, you don't have to make excuses, give reasons, or justify yourself. This is important to state because we've been trained the opposite way. We think we have to justify, excuse, and give reasons. These weaken our boundaries. An uncompromising no strengthens them.

As a legal nurse consultant you will need to give this conscious attention because we are trained to be helpers and people who will serve others. One of the elements of nursing says that you should be selfless and give and give and give.

Many of us grew up in nursing at a time that nurses were expected to continually say yes to the extra shift or the double time or giving up a vacation time or working an extra weekend. There was a lot of guilt associated with trying to say no to those requests. That carries over into working with attorneys because they often have last minute requests and needs that legal nurse consultants really try very hard to meet. But some of those requests, particularly the last-minute ones, are unreasonable.

I know personally that we struggled with this when I ran my company. The instances when we said yes when we should've said no often resulted in difficulties in getting paid and a variety of problems until we developed a formula so that we could very effectively deal with last minute requests. We had to learn to be especially firm with people who didn't want to pay but wanted the work done last minute and then would try to come up with some excuses to why they didn't have to pay.

It's definitely an issue for nurses because of the way that we are conditioned to try to help other people.

You may be thinking of situations in which "NO" didn't seem to be an option. Sometimes circumstances, not people, cause the overwhelm.

That kind of situation means we have to look at the circumstances and weigh all of the different options. Using the tool of awareness, ask yourself, "Now what?" This means looking at all the aspects of the situation with care.

If you realize that you can feel a "NO" there, you may have told yourself that you're obligated to the situation. Ask yourself if it's a self-imposed obligation. Ask if you are willing to let go of this or if you still have some attachment to it.

If it's not a clear "YES," it's a "NO," and we go back to our guidelines of awareness and responsibility. You may notice something new about your boundaries. You may discover that some things you're currently saying "YES" to are things to which you'd like to start saying "NO."

Think now of some things that you'd like to start saying "NO" to in your business or in your life.

It could be a volunteer activity.

It could be working overtime.

It could be an attorney who wants a discount.

When asked this question, people may say, "Working no more than 45 hours a week at my day job." If that's the case, it means you decide that at a certain time you'll be leaving for the day because you have commitments elsewhere.

Others say, "Demands of others and not enough time for myself." This means that you need to say a big NO to making yourself last on the list.

Some people realize they need to say no to people or circumstances that kill time. This takes awareness. You may be talking to people and realize that they are going to suck your time and energy. The responsibility part activates when you say "You know, thanks, but no thanks."

The Trickster's Triangle

Let's look at the elephant from a different angle. A psychologist named Stephen Karpman did some research on internal states that led to certain kinds of relationships. The idea is that whatever programs are running through your mind, your internal conversations and expectations help to form how you relate with others.

A style of coaching called Radical Leadership calls this the Trickster's Triangle. This model represents three archetypes. You'll find the dynamics of the relationships within it part of every Hollywood blockbuster. These movies are popular in part because they represent something that's a factor in our lives, even if we're not fully aware of it.

These three archetypes are "the villain" "the victim" and "the hero." I will describe each of these in detail so that we can see how they play out in the real world.

Each of these three different archetypes is unable to meet people on an equal basis. Instead, they use their particular tactics to manipulate others in order to get what they want.

The Villain

"The villains" are people who are so afraid of being powerless that they overpower people. They always have the effect of making somebody else or something else bad or wrong. The theme of their role in interactions is "… you idiot."

They're not bad or wrong. They are doing the best they can to protect themselves and get what they want. The villains you've met in your life could be somebody at work, a doctor that you've run up against, or an attorney that you've consulted with or thought about consulting with. They may say things to you that have the undertone of "You idiot."

A similar personality disorder is called "the Borderline Personality." In that syndrome the person tends to set up the situation of idealizing another person and then figuring out a way to bring them down a peg or knock them off the pedestal. You hear, "You're so wonderful," but then all of a sudden you become "You idiot" in that person's mind. It's a tricky situation and can be quite disheartening to the person who doesn't see the trap coming.

I got caught up in a trap about 20 years ago when I got into a partnership with another LNC. I gave her a project to work on, thinking we would equally share in the financial rewards. She took over the project, completely redid it, and then told me it belonged to her from then on. I was astounded by the trick that she pulled. She took something away from me that I never intended to lose and justified it as a "business decision."

When I realized what she had done, I called a friend of mine who was a psychiatric nurse practitioner and asked, "What just happened here?" She said, "Oh, she's a borderline personality." I said, "I feel so stupid because I didn't recognize it." She said, "Don't feel stupid. Richard Nixon was a borderline personality. He pulled the wool over the American people's eyes and created borderline personality scenarios."

I'd like you to take a moment now and see what comes to mind when you think of "villain." Write down some words or phrases.

People have responded to this questions in a variety of ways. Some say that the villain says, "I will not approve your request because you don't need this" or "Do it because I said so." I think we can hear the parental voice here.

Some people say, "I shut down around villains and start avoiding." Others observe that they have a couple of villains at work.

We've all met villains. And sometimes they live inside us. Think of internal dialogues you may have had where you're telling yourself, "I can't believe you did that." Do you hear the "you idiot" in that?

Be alert to villains showing up. Sometimes their strategies are very subtle.

The Victim

People who try to retreat from villains are likely to be victims.

"Victims" are afraid of power, so they'll push it away whenever it appears.

- "It's not me."
- "It's not mine."

- "I didn't know better."
- "It wasn't my job."

What they basically do is give up any kind of power and whine, "Poor me." I don't say this as a judgment. It's not bad and wrong. We want to look at the impact of this personality type.

I heard an expression when I was growing up. It was, "You Can't Fight City Hall." I remember the first time I fought City Hall and I won. I was astounded because I had been taught from the time I was little that you can't be victorious and you can't take on powerful people because you're just a victim.

Think of some of the comments you've heard victims make. Do they remove themselves from any conversation that contains conflict? Do they give up and give in?

- Are there any victims you've met at work?
- "It's not my fault."
- "I didn't know better."

What kinds of things do you hear? Here are some examples

- "You threw me under the bus."
- "I can't believe you did that."
- "Why did you do that?"

People who detach from anyone who doesn't support them are likely to be victims. Another phrase to look for is, "Poor me. It always happens to me. It never fails." Also consider this one: "I thought we were friends."

Here are some more.

- "Why me?"
- "Poor me."

Always some external factor is happening to the victim or disturbing the peace.

The Hero

The hero actually powers up and lifts up other people. A lot of heroes will be "YES" people. They'll say, "Yes, I can handle that. I've got it," and are swooping in and saving the day.

These are the kinds of people who will take on extra shifts because a staffer is sick again or didn't show up to work again because she's ill or having a family problem. They always present themselves this way: "I'll save you" or "I can handle this" or "Don't worry, I've got it."

What are some of the phrases that you've heard or maybe you've made as a hero? Do you recognize these phrases?

- "No problem, how can I help?"
- "What seems like a small step is really a giant leap."

An important feature of the hero is that people who act this way have such a need to be important that they may disempower people that they work with.

Role Players Need Each Other

Based on these descriptions, you can see that each of these pieces interact with the others. It may not surprise you that a villain needs a victim, but the victim also needs the villain in order to fulfill her own personality type.

To emphasize how important it is not to judge or blame, I'm going to share that as a manager, I often played "the hero" role to come in and solve problems—perhaps at times when my employees should have been given the opportunity to solve the problem themselves.

Here are some more examples.

Connecting with really powerful people: Powerful people may interact with you as if they are the villain. They like to wield their power sword. They may put you on the defensive and make you into a victim.

Negotiating contracts: Be on high alert while negotiating contracts. Villains will habitually try to manipulate the negotiations to get the kind of contract they want. It's important to stop them and to set up your boundaries.

Working with difficult clients: Difficult clients who keep asking for more and more and more or always have that last minute emergency again and again and again may play the role of victim.

This is a good place to remind you that these behavior patterns operate both externally and internally. Be mindful of that part of you that wants to play victim or hero. Women and nurses fix things. They make the peace even when it means not getting what they want.

If you notice any such patterns in yourself, notice them

without judging. Evaluate all mental and physical patterns on the basis of what works. If it does, keep it. If it doesn't, look for a different solution.

Party Time

The reason Dr. Eric Berne called his book *Games People Play* was because that's what role players turn relationships into. One way they do this is to invite you to a party.

If you get an invitation to an ordinary party, you see if you're available, you decide if you think you'll like the people at the party, and then you respond.

At a Trickster's Triangle party, you're being invited to play a role. In negotiations, a villain may be inviting you to become a victim. He wants you to be willing to take a lower amount of money, to mentally devalue your services, or agree to do something that doesn't fit into the range of your services because he's scared or bullied you into this position.

This means you need to be aware of what's going on beneath the surface. You think you're talking about financial arrangements, but a would-be villain is looking for someone to dominate, someone he can make an idiot.

This game can be played in a very subtle way; that's why you need to be so aware. If you ever feel like people come to the negotiation table, and they're trying to scare you into signing a contract, it's more important than ever for you to be a clear "YES" or a clear "NO." You need to choose.

Here's an example from my experience. An attorney got an invoice from us for the services of one of our experts. She did a great job with a large amount of records, and she gave him the report that he needed. He wasn't unhappy with her conclusions, and he wasn't unhappy with her credentials. He said to me, "Well, this is a pretty big invoice. What can we do about it? Can you work with me on this?" I said, "Sure, I can give you a payment plan." He asked, "What can we do to reduce it?" and I said, "Nothing."

He tried a few more pointed questions. I basically answered each response, and then I waited. He was kind of flabbergasted at the end of the phone call because the invoice was still in effect. There was no reason for me to reduce it, and he ultimately paid it. His approach was, "Work with me on the invoice," and my approach was, "I don't plan to." I reiterated her great credentials and how much material she had to go through and that she met his deadline. He agreed that all of that was true, but he just didn't want to pay that high a bill.

Obviously in the past his pressure tactics had worked. He'd successfully manipulated people into giving him what he wanted. People probably even thought there might be something wrong with that invoice.

Learning to set clear boundaries will help you whether you're a brand-new legal nurse consultant, have a little experience, or are an expert. You can learn to say "YES" or "NO" at any point in your career.

You will also learn that if you say too many "YESes" that you will end up feeling overwhelmed and frustrated.

I invite you to take a moment to think about some of the invitations you've accepted in the past. Maybe you ignored your boundaries because you wanted to save someone, and it ended up costing you more time than you'd anticipated. Maybe because you gave one "YES," someone else expected "YESes" forever after.

If you're having trouble thinking of examples, remember how deceptive these invitations are. They can, in fact, be very inviting. You don't see the trap in them. Also, without judgment or guilt, think about how you may have really wanted to say "YES."

One good example is a last-minute rush job. You will run into that request a lot. You've got to be very clear with these ones. You've got to be very clear with your "YES" or "NO." You may find that one approach is to have a fee for rush jobs. It has to be an amount that makes the job worth it. That's a great way to set your boundaries.

Awareness and Responsibility Revisited

Here are three keys to dealing with game-playing invitations.

Do not accept the invitations that they're putting out for you to join them on the triangle. Just simply choose NO. It's an invitation, not an order.

However, you'll have to remember that you've probably been trained into whatever your particular role is. Also remember that you've probably trained others to see you in that role and to approach you while playing their roles. You might be a hero who rescues your employees from trouble. Don't be surprised if you have one or more employees who come to you in tears frequently, crying about the latest disaster, and begging for your help.

Second, be clear on your "YESes" and "NOs."

Sound familiar? I'll say it one more time. Be clear on your "YESes" and "NOs." If you walk away with that, I'll be happy.

Asking For What You Want

This is the last piece of the puzzle. As you apply awareness and responsibility, and learn to be alert for game players, you develop the confidence to ask for what you want. Since you're a legal nurse consultant, one of the things you most want is to land contracts with ease.

Ask yourself, on a scale from 1 to 5, how easy it is to ask for what you want. 1 means you really struggle. 5 means that you ask effortlessly. This is an important thing for you to notice.

Having asked you that question, I'm going to quickly follow up with another. Ask yourself how attached you are to the answer when you ask for something.

It's an interesting question from the negotiation standpoint. If an attorney senses that a legal nurse consultant really desperately wants and needs the work, that weakens the position of the LNC when attorneys are asking for some concessions or negotiate the hourly rate or some other aspect of the fee agreement.

If they feel like they can manipulate you and manipulate you, and you give, give, give, they'll do that. And you still might not get the contract. An attorney might say, "Even though you've given me everything you want, I found somebody else that I want to work with."

Why is that? Powerful people want to work with other powerful people. When you set firm boundaries, they will respect you. They will admire your clarity and believe that you bring the same kind of precision and focus to your work. Even so-called villains may be relieved when they can give up their games. It's hard work to keep them going. They like knowing what's acceptable and not acceptable with you.

This is the beauty of adding detachment to awareness, responsibility, and having a keen eye for game playing.

Learning Detachment

You need to practice detachment. Here's a suggestion that can make asking for what you want easier. It has to do with how you feel when you ask. Imagine you're asking, and inside you're anxious and uneasy and thinking how awful it will be if the other person says, "No." These thoughts and feelings reduce the likelihood of a positive response.

I've mentioned that I used to be involved in a multilevel marketing organization. In it I learned that every "NO" brings you closer to a "YES." If you can learn to believe this, you can be unfazed by the "NOs" and delighted by the "YESes."

This may not come easily to you, and here again creating an affirmation may help you to release attachment. You could say, "When someone says NO, they're not saying NO to me."

You could use what I learned; every NO leads to a YES.

What you don't want to do is to manipulate anyone into a "YES" because that puts you into game playing.

Awareness will tell you when you're attached. Notice how it feels. You may experience it as a stranglehold. It's not good for you, and it's not good for your business.

Our society as a whole has been taught not to want things because it's selfish, so when you want something, it means it's close to your heart. From my heart I want a thriving business. I want to work with people who respect me and respect my boundaries. If this guy is trying to manipulate me, maybe we're not a good fit together. If he continues to disrespect my boundaries, then maybe I don't want to work with him because he's just going to continue to do that when we're in a relationship together.

It's crucial that you know what you want from your heart so that you can ask for it and be unattached, not just for you and your business but because it's in service of them and their business and what they're trying to create and make happen. This will mean that you don't have to manipulate them or work hard or bend over backwards or blur the lines of your boundaries at all. But you know that you can support them, and then they'll hire you at whatever rate you believe you're worth. To recap, the four keys to dealing with powerful people, combating overwhelm, and attracting clients with ease are:

First, "Happiness first." We talked about this in the beginning. If you focus on "How do I get the money?" or "How do I get the clients?" you will start to become attached to your clients or their money. But if you focus on what authentically makes you happy, and do what makes you happy, and create boundaries that make you happy, people will automatically be attracted to you.

Second, do not accept the invitations that they're putting out for you to jump on the triangle. You will encounter people on the triangle. We all have a reticular activating system, which means when something is brought to our attention, our new awareness makes us notice it much more. It may seem like we're running into it everywhere. It was always there, but before we didn't notice it.

Third, be clear on your "YESes" and "NOs." If it is not a clear yes then make it a no.

Fourth, ask for what you want and be unattached.

Now the big question is, "What do you want?" If you don't know, and you don't have a clear compass of where you're headed, it's important that you take the time to build awareness around that and create it so that you know what you want in your business and for your life.

I'll give you one final piece of advice. Now that you've read this chapter, read it again in a few days. Begin to look at your business and your life from its perspectives. Look deeper. You'll find answers you didn't expect and wisdom that you perhaps didn't know you had.

CHAPTER 3

Developing Your Business

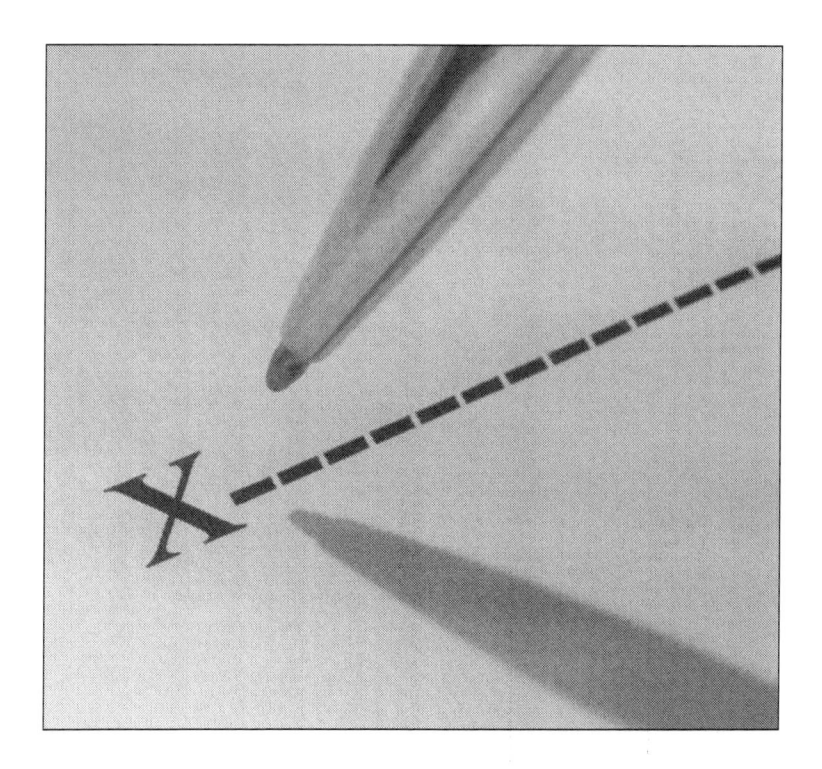

CHAPTER 3

Developing Your Business

Nurses come into legal nurse consulting from many starting points. Some have no experience in the field; others may be working in related fields or roles that fit within legal nurse consulting. Such nurses may not have applied the label of "legal nurse consulting" to their practice. For example, they could be doing risk management, onsite evaluations of facilities, workers compensation case management, life care planning, or other roles.

Full-Time or Part-Time

Some nurses become burned out in their jobs, get tired of commuting, or dealing with the politics of nursing administration. They look at legal nurse consulting as the solution. Make no mistake about it — starting a business is *work!* But it is work of a different type.

Many nurses hold onto their full-time jobs and begin a business part-time. A lot of people will try to hang onto a clinical job where they're working two or three days a week. Maybe they're working in the float pool, and they try to do their business as a sideline. This model works for many nurses. No matter how you start your business, you have to say, "I'm committed to starting this business, and therefore I'm going to invest my time, energy, and money into it."

Others save money until they have enough to pay bills for six months and then take the plunge and leave their full-time jobs. This approach requires you to invest in your business, and that means your time, your energy, and your money. Maybe it's a matter of working really hard and working a lot of overtime in the beginning to save up some capital. Then you may get to that point where you say, "Today's the deadline, and today I'm actually going to do this for real. It's going to be a make-it or break-it type situation." You might need to take out a loan or find a family member who would help support you. That gives you a period of time to really commit to your business and make a go of it.

Under this model, you will say to yourself, "Okay, I'm going to give it all I've got. I've got six months of income to do it, and if all else fails, I have another plan." Make that commitment and jump in with both feet.

Many people never get their LNC business off the ground because they're busy working 36 hours a week at the hospital and halfway trying to build their business the other four days a week. It can be hard to market and make sales calls or return attorneys' calls while working in a clinical role. Ultimately, it is difficult for part-time business owners to invest as much into their business development as they do working the 36 hours a week for their employer. Can you create a situation where you invest more in your own business than you do in your employer's business?

What Are Your Skills?

Anyone who wants to start or grow a business has to examine the motivation. What is your passion? What are you passionate about, and why do you want to start a legal nurse consulting business? What do you like to do with your spare time? Do you have certain skills that you've developed or learned that set you apart from someone else? What do other people say about you? How do they describe you? Do they describe you as a business person? Are you analytical? Are you detail oriented? Can you communicate well orally and in writing? I see these as prerequisites for success in legal nurse consulting.

Does your family encourage you in your business plan? Your family's going to have to be able to support you—not necessarily financially but emotionally support your business endeavor so that you aren't battling that at home while you're trying to get this business off the ground. Roles and responsibilities have a way of changing when a family member is in business. Other family members may resist the changes.

If you're a self-starter, if you can get along with different personalities, particularly if you're good at making decisions, those things make you a good business owner. You also have to have the physical and emotional stamina to run a business because it's a lot of work. The joke is "I work half a day, which 12 hours do I work?"

I met a father of four small boys at a time when my oldest son was about five. He said to me, "Oh, your husband owns his own business. That means he sets his own hours." I said, "Yeah, let me tell you about it. He works from about 7:00 in the morning until 7:00 at night and every weekend and there's nobody there to tell him to go home." We went on and had a discussion. By the time I was done he was beginning to back away from me. He said, "Hmm, maybe there are some things that I hadn't really considered."

Being self-employed requires a dedication and a hard-working philosophy that may surprise people who are seeing it from the outside.

You have to have a strong drive, be able to define your personal needs and strengths, and know your financial objectives. Do you want to get this business off the ground because you're interested in money? Is it flexibility you are after? Everyone's definition of success is different. Some people want to start their own business because they see a glossy ad stating they can make $XXX an hour. Other people want to have the flexibility to be home with school-aged children.

You have to define those priorities and then stay focused on those before you know if you're going to be cut out for business.

Define the Nature of Your Services

There are many business models for legal nurse consultants. Do you want to:

- testify as an expert witness?
- be a non-testifying consultant?
- work on Medicare Set Aside allocations?
- be a case manager?
- supply expert witnesses? be a life care planner?

If you are open to different roles, you will find out what works and where you make the most money. As you get busy, you narrow your focus. You concentrate on areas that are more lucrative so that the time invested in that particular area is more valuably spent.

Also be open to different types of cases. There are medical issues in criminal, toxic tort, product liability, pharmaceutical, and matrimonial cases. Many LNCs think exclusively in terms of medical and nursing malpractice and personal injury cases and overlook those other types of cases. Be open to the kinds of attorneys you will work with. I interviewed one nurse who wanted to work as my employee. She said, "I would never want to help plaintiff attorneys." She quickly realized that she could not take that position and work with me, since many of our clients were plaintiff attorneys.

When your work is diversified, this helps you better manage your business.

Foundations of Business

There are essential legal and financial components of starting any business.

Business Structure
Seek out an attorney who specializes in helping business start-ups. Learn about your choices of business structure, such as setting up an S corporation, C corporation or LLC (Limited Liability Company). Time invested in exploring these options will help you select the right structure for your business.

Determine a name for your business that is not already in use in your state. (You can find out if the name you want is registered by checking with the Department of State in your state.) Select a name that is compelling and explains the services you have to offer. For example, suppose your name is John Bell and you provide legal nurse consulting services. "John Bell Consulting" does not provide your potential market with an understanding of what you offer. "Bell Legal Nurse Consulting" is a clearer alternative.

Once you have determined the name of the company, register it with the Department of State. Your business attorney or local county courthouse should be able to assist you with this, or you may be able to do it online.

Partnerships

Many people find having a business partner an appealing way to start a business. An attorney once described a partnership to me as a "marriage without the sex." When a partnership works well, you are able to capitalize on each other's strengths and experiences.

Your harmony helps your business succeed. You pool your talents, and your hard work combines to create a solid venture. You develop trust in each other. Your creativity creates a more solid company.

Partnerships do not always succeed. The impact can be like a divorce. They can fail for a variety of reasons, such as:

1. There is an inequitable amount of work or money invested in the company. One partner feels he or she is contributing a disproportionate amount of resources.
2. The life circumstances of one of the partners changes.

3. A business venture is no longer possible or appealing.
4. The partners develop conflicts that cannot be resolved.

My only experience with a partner was not positive. We developed a conflict that we could not resolve. It cost me thousands of dollars in legal fees to separate from my partner. The legal fees swamped the profits of our business. In looking back at the painful lessons learned, I see a few things I should have done differently. The primary lesson was that I should have known my partner much better than I did when I developed the relationship and plans for our business venture. There were personality issues that torpedoed our venture and doomed it before its start. I now stress that you should know your partner well before creating a company with that person.

Financial Structure

Seek a knowledgeable accountant to help you set up your financial structure. You should be aware of what records you need to keep, the taxes you need to pay, and how to best manage your money so you have a workable cash flow. Keep your personal money separate from your business money. For example, have a company credit card so you can easily track expenses.

Consulting practices may have an ebb and flow of money but your need to pay rent and utilities is constant.

One of the mantras of business owners is: "Businesses more frequently fail because of lack of cash flow than from lack of work." Do not take on expensive overhead in the beginning of your business before you can more accurately predict cash flow. Look for ways to economize, run the business out of your house, and get used furniture and office equipment.

You can always upgrade when your business demands it and can fund it. My first desk was a board placed over two filing cabinets!

It is a good idea to periodically change accountants or have an outside accountant evaluate your business operations. That person may see something your primary accountant has missed.

Database

I wouldn't be able to run my businesses without a database. Also known as a client relationship management system, your database is something that you will use in putting together information about your contacts. The one that I rely on in is called ACT! by Sage. It is easy to customize. It is designed to be able to keep track of all of our clients. It keeps track of all of the experts I used in my business. It also kept track of our vendors. We entered every case into ACT!

ACT! is for individuals and small business companies and a variety of industries. It's for people who want to organize their contact information, manage their daily responsibilities, and communicate more effectively to improve production. It organized my business.

We set up groups in ACT! We had groups of expert witnesses; we had groups of attorney clients. We used ACT! to do mailings to everybody in the group by having it connected through our email system. We also set alarms to follow up on items. When we sent out a case to an expert witness, we set an alarm for 3 weeks later to make sure that we contacted that person to find out the status of the review.

We customized all of the fields to make sense for what we do. For example, we had a field that identified the allegation in a case. It might be a medical malpractice case with an allegation of a failure to diagnose. We had a drop down list that we customized with the potential causes of action. We could find all of the cases in which there was a delay in diagnosis allegation or all of the car accident cases or all of the criminal cases. It's a very versatile program that has a lot of capability for customization.

A database puts all your vital information in one easy- to-access location. In one software program, you should have every email, every phone call, all the documents they sent you, complete to-do lists, meeting schedules, and reminders. It leaves no task undone. It allows you to make decisions in a more successful way to advance your relationships with your clients. When people call you, and you look at that person's record, you know what the last email said or what your last conversation was. It really helps grow that personal business relationship.

There are other database program besides ACT! There's one called Goldmine that is also contact relationship software. Daylite is one for Mac computer users. A good database integrates with your emails, correspondence, saves form letters, and has a place to keep notes. It helps you keep track of all your phone calls, calendars, any projects you're working on, and any opportunities that this client may offer you. You should be able to set up groups so you can quickly find information.

When I contacted an attorney and we were talking about cases, I could open up his record and flip through and say, "What happened to the Rogers case? What's going on with that?" Or the attorney will call me and say, "I don't know if you remember me," and I say, "Sure. We worked on the Rogers case in 2010." And he'll say, "Oh, you have such a good memory." I'd say, "I have a database."

Are there substitutes for a database? In my opinion, no. If you are using a contact or address form, you are not using a client relationship management system because you just can't keep track of your business relationships in that type of software, or in an Excel spreadsheet. It is the only method to effectively manage your business.

Business Card

You have established your legal and financial structure and invested in a database. You are now ready to design your business card. Your business card also is a way to market your services. This is not a part of your business development where you should try to save pennies. For example, there are a number of business cards that you can purchase that are part of brochures, but they look homemade. Carry your cards by the dozens and always have them with you. Put them in your car, briefcase, wallet, or wherever you can grab them in a moment.

It is important to invest in a well-designed business card. Some people use the space on the back of the business card to list services, social media details, or QR Codes. Some people keep it blank in order to allow the person who receives the business card to take notes on the material. Here are some points to consider when designing a business card:

- Make sure you don't have a glossy surface on your card. It is very hard to write on.

- Use white or cream colored paper. Dark paper will not scan well and also prevents the recipient from being able to make a note on it. Print on dark paper is also often hard to read.
- Make sure it is easy to find the essential information, including your name, address, phone, fax, and social media details.
- Provide a bit of information to indicate what your business is about.
- Have someone proofread your card. It has to be error-free.

Email

Your email address should be professional and reflect your company name. Avoid cute names or those that clearly refer to another aspect of your life, such as adamsmom@hotmail.com.

Set up your signature lines to be automatically added to each message in your email account. Your email signature should include your complete name, educational degrees, phone number, city, and state.

This will help your email recipients know what time zone you are in. Include your web address, social media addresses, and your tag line. Your tag line reflects the services you provide, for example, legal nurse consulting services. Add your picture to your settings in your email. It creates a more personal feeling.

Your Professional Look

Your letterhead, business card, brochures and website should be designed to be consistent. The same logo, color scheme, and look should carry through. Try to keep your font consistent throughout these items for uniformity. The masthead for your letterhead should be designed in a professional way and look consistent with your business card. If possible, look at the letterheads of your ideal clients and see if you can replicate that same type of professional feel. When I started Med League, I noticed that most of the attorneys were using cream colored paper for their letterhead, so I used that type of paper for our letterhead. I used blue letters to provide a little bit of color. Blue is also a color that many people associate with truthfulness, honesty, and calmness. By mirroring the clients that you're currently doing business with and wish to attract, you give the subliminal appearance that you're just like them. The cliché, "people like people that are like themselves" is appropriate for this example.

Website

Prospective clients will expect you to have a website. This address will appear on your business card and letterhead. Even if you just have a one-page information site that lists your contact information and a list of services, it is imperative that you have some type of web presence.

In chapter 6, I will share more with you about websites. I devote two chapters to the topics of legal nurse consultant websites and blogging in the second book in this series: *Legal Nurse Consultant Marketing*. See **www.legalnursebusiness.com** for details.

Chapter 4

Getting Your First Case

CHAPTER 4:

Getting Your First Case

There are many ways to start and grow a business. This chapter describes one way to add cold calls into your marketing plan. Some people find them to be useful marketing and prospecting tools.

The Marketing Mindset

As I discussed in Chapter 1, your mindset is a huge factor in your success. Some people thrive on cold calls. A cold call occurs when you contact a person without having a previous relationship with him. Many people have heard of cold calls, received cold calls, and want nothing to do with cold calls. An understanding of the techniques that convert cold calls to clients can help those who are resistant to cold calls to appreciate the doors this marketing method can open.

Part of the marketing mindset is rooted in recognizing how you as a nurse can contribute to the legal team.

Think about what you have to offer to an attorney. You are a registered nurse with years of experience in health care and with medical records. You understand various types of injuries, illnesses, disease processes, and the healthcare system. Your mindset changes from a sales person making a "cold call" to being a nurse who is going to educate someone else about a process or an injury. You can interpret that pile of records sitting on the attorney's desk that he really didn't quite understand. This makes you very valuable to him in working his case.

Research

Create a list of law firms (prospects) so that each day you will have a different place to try to conquer. Do your homework ahead of time, and identify the law firm as the kind of practice that can hire you. They should be working on the types of cases that will cause them to value having a nurse to help them interpret the records. Make sure that they are not doing employment law or real estate but actually do cases that involve a personal injury, professional negligence, or a product liability case.

Review the Martindale.com listing as well as the firm website. Doing that homework and knowing who you want to target is important. Create lists of prospects with phone numbers and addresses.

Marketing can consume an enormous amount of resources. A non-targeted approach can end up costing you a lot of money. Be clear about your ideal prospects. Do you want to work with only defense attorneys? Are you targeting plaintiff firms? Do you want to work with firms within a certain geographic radius? Do you want small to midsize firms as your clients? How can you get these answers? Martindale.com is a useful resource.

Your state's American Association of Justice will have primarily plaintiff attorneys as their members. The Defense Research Institute attracts the other side of the bar. Both groups offer annual and periodic educational programs for attorneys and paralegals. You may be permitted to attend their programs. The bar association in your state may also offer local and annual meetings.

Investigate these programs and go prepared with your business cards.

Build a relationship with the people who are the most likely to make good referrals for you. Identify those people. Your referral sources may be other legal vendors or attorneys in your social circle, church, and neighborhood.

What is the checklist for a good prospect? Who is a good A level prospect? Check your criteria against the prospect list you are currently using. We have to find out who are the most important people to target and how are we going to get in the door. Concentrate on only those prospects who deserve to be on your list.

That may not be easy. Take a look at the clients that you have who are currently "A level" clients and identify some of the commonalities as to why they're "A level" clients for you. They may buy the right amount of services; they may buy it at the right price and in the right timeframe. Are they in a certain type of law practice? Are they in a certain geographical area; are the people at a certain level?

Also, what is it about the firms that make them more right for you than others? Are they facing certain issues that would make them need your services more than other firms would? It's almost like taking a pencil and sharpening it until you have a very, fine point. All the shavings fall away, and you know exactly who it is who belongs on your list. The people who are on your list should be people you are anxious to do business with. Once you have your list, dive deeper into the data.

You can warm up a cold situation, or a cold call, with some research. You can do some research on a company or a person and make the message much more customized so the cold call doesn't feel quite so cold anymore. You need to know what you're going to say when you connect with your prospect.

Do some research about the firm and the decision maker. You can Google the firm and find out what's been going on, whether there are press releases that have been sent out not too long ago. Be careful when you Google. Things on the Internet live forever. You may be reading something, and it looks really good, and it may be from five years ago. So pay attention to the dates.

Targeting the Decision Maker

There is a process to streamlining your way to the decision maker. The decision maker in a law firm may be a solo practitioner, a managing partner, or a partner. The first thing you need to do is find out who you're going to target. Once you know who you're going to target, you need to know what you're going to say, which is, of course, the message. You could be the best seller in the world and completely waste your time if you're calling the wrong people or if you have no idea what to say when you reach the decision maker.

You should study the prospect firm's website. Be careful with dates here, but you can find out a lot about an attorney this way. You can find out what college that person went to and whether the two of you have anything in common. All that makes for a very good customized message. In the legal world, when attorneys have the opportunity to brag about their large dollar verdicts or their wins, that gets on their websites pretty quickly. They also tend to have a profile of every attorney who works in the office with their picture and where they went to school and their area of practice. It is rare to find a law firm that doesn't have a website.

Once you know the kinds of law firms that belong on your target list, the next thing to do is to drop in the name of the correct decision maker. If you're not sure who is the right person, start with that person's boss. If you're not sure who that person's boss is, start at the very top of the company and work your way down. Don't start at the bottom and work your way up. The top attorney in the firm may be identified as a managing partner.

The decision maker is usually a high-level person and very busy. It's really important to understand what's going on in your prospect's work-life that's going to affect the way he or she reacts to you when you call or when you email. This is a person who spends most likely a lot of time in meetings. He or she is meeting with clients, taking depositions, or trying cases. They're looking at their email or they're listening to voicemail, so they're very distracted. That's important to understand when you're leaving a voicemail for somebody. You need to be very clear and concise and say only what matters.

Timing for Making Calls

Time of Day
There are certain times of the day that are much better than others to reach your decision maker — 7:30 a.m.-9:00 a.m. 12:00 p.m.-1:00 p.m., and of course any time after 5:00 p.m. If you want your decision maker to hear the message without the assistant interrupting, consider leaving the decision maker the message on a Sunday night. That way he or she may come in first thing Monday morning, before the assistant comes in, and hear the voice mail. Your message will say, "If you could go ahead and give permission to your assistant to put a time on the calendar, I'll call back after 9:00 a.m. Sometimes when you call the assistant after 9:00 a.m., that person will say "Yes, Tom Smith told me to put this on the calendar." That can be very successful.

Day of the Week
There's no bad day of the week to make calls. No one day is better than another, no one day worse than another. Try your calls at all different times. Every decision maker has different work habits, a different process that he or she goes through. Record when you make the calls because when you're calling a lot of people, there's no way for you to remember that a month ago you caught them live at 5:15 p.m. on a Friday unless you mark that down in your database.

In some states there is something in the legal system called the *motion day*. In New Jersey every other Friday the attorneys are in the courtroom if they have motions to argue and there are no trials taking place on those days. You will have a greater chance of reaching an attorney on a motion day because if he or she has no motions to argue, that person's more likely to be in the office. I don't know if all states have motion days, but that is something that legal nurse consultants might want to ask their clients — "Do you have motion days and when are they?" Then once you know the pattern you can plan accordingly in terms of trying to reach your prospects.

Time of Year

There are certain times of the year that are very good for reaching decision makers live that most people don't think about. The first one is August. There are many people who do go away for vacation, but no one goes away for four weeks. So if you don't reach them in week 1 or 2, you'll probably reach them in week 3 or 4. Most firm meetings aren't happening at that time, so people are at their desks and relaxed.

Also during the week between Christmas and New Year's, not everyone goes away, so the ones who are at their desks are pretty chatty. They may not see you that week but if you ask them for a time next year, which is all of maybe four days away, their calendars are usually wide open. People who wait until after January to ask for time on a calendar usually end up waiting till the end of January because the calendar is already filled up.

Frequency

Never give up on efforts to reach your prospect. Unless you learn something about your prospect that leads you to believe he or she is no longer a good prospect for you, keep going. Be persistent, be respectful and be patient, and you will get your turn. Your competition will not hang in that long. You know that there are certain prospects that are going to take a long time to reach. But if you get in to see those people and you end up doing business with them, it can be very worthwhile.

So if you only have those kinds of people on your list, you better believe your sales cycle is going to be very long. If you have some of those people on your list and some of the other people who are easier to penetrate on your list, then you'll have some that become your clients now. You'll close sales on the others later. But you'll be filling your pipeline with the big ones as well as the medium to small ones that will close a little sooner.

Start at the Top and Work Your Way Down

Set priorities with your prospect list. The most important ones should be at the top of your list. Work your way down. This same philosophy goes for when you're penetrating an organization. Start at the top and work your way down. You will get much further when you talk to the assistant to the partner than you do when you talk to the receptionist.

If you're planning to create a call list, do not start with the A's. Start with right around G or you can start with Z and work your way backwards. Why? Because when your competition did the same thing, they started at A and by D they gave up.

Talking to the Gatekeeper

The gatekeeper may be the person who answers the phone, or the attorney's secretary or paralegal. Ask the gatekeeper, "Do you use legal nurse consultants?" Use your well-rehearsed script. Some of the people answering the phone will refer your question to a legal secretary or paralegal, who may be intrigued and want to set up an appointment for you to meet with the attorneys. Spend a good deal of time with the person who answers the phone right from the very beginning, so that you can sell him or her that you have a value to the attorney. Your goal is to have that person help you set up those appointments.

A lot of people struggle with this and their impression of the gatekeeper is that this person is very much like a bouncer. The gatekeeper can be very helpful if you think about what this person has access to. This person has access to your decision maker's calendar and your decision maker. Think about how often your decision maker walks past the assistant all day long. When you have trouble reaching the decision maker directly, contact the assistant and open up communication with that person. Say "If I sent you an email with some information, would you mind sending it to Tom Smith?"

Remember that the assistant is instructions-oriented, and task-oriented. If you give him a task, he will most likely do it. So the assistant will usually say "Sure, send me the email and I'll forward it." You say, "Terrific. I'll give you a call tomorrow and see if Tom Smith said it's okay to put a time on his calendar to come on in and meet with him next week.

Meanwhile, Tom Smith takes a look at the email, and if he doesn't, the assistant says, "Have you had a chance to look at the email because the nurse said she's calling tomorrow." So the assistant will remind Tom to do this, and then the next day the assistant will say, "Is it okay to put the nurse on the calendar because I know she's calling?" You'll get a yes or a no that way and sometimes an appointment without ever having spoken with the decision maker. But that's okay, because we did a lot of qualifying before we put the prospect list together. This is how we view the assistant. Not like a bouncer but somebody who's just incredibly helpful for us.

Leaving Voice Mails

The person who answers the phone may simply identify what you are calling about and direct your call to the attorney's voice mail. Be prepared for what you plan to say. Leave a voice mail for the attorney. These people are busy, and so it may take some time to get on their radar. Be respectful; be politely persistent. It's almost like being a constant presence in this person's work life until this person is ready to get on the phone with you.

When you leave a message, there are two pieces of the message that are important. The first one is content. The content has got to be relevant, compelling, and in language that resonates with the decision maker. You also want to tailor it to your target audience.

Delivery

The next piece of the message is delivery. This is the one people tend to overlook. They do spend time on the content but sometimes they forget about the delivery.

Delivery is very important; modulate your tone and cadence and, most importantly, be conversational. How do you sound when you leave voicemails? Leave 10 voicemails for yourself. After each one, pick it up and hear how you sound and pretend you're your prospect — busy all day long, just came back from three meetings, about to go to a few more, and distracted.

What's coming through? If you were your prospect, would you give you a meeting? And if the answer to that isn't yes, you need some more work. Here are some tips on how to be more conversational. The first thing is you should have the sentences you believe are the most important in front of you. You should know them well enough that you don't have to read them. If you're finding that you don't sound conversational, flip your paper over and don't read from the paper. If you still find that you're not as conversational as you'd like to be, stand up and get some more air going through your body; sometimes that changes everything. Prepare ahead of time. Write your script and practice it over and over until you can say it flawlessly. Practice in front of the mirror, practice with your spouse, children, or pet. Practice in the car.

If you are still not as conversational as you want to be, talk to a mirror so it looks like you're smiling. Or put a picture of somebody else on your wall. You can pretend you're just talking to somebody else. So now you sound very conversational as opposed to sounding practiced and rehearsed. Once you're ready, rehearse until it doesn't sound rehearsed.

Structure of a Voice Mail

Here are a few models for leaving voice mails.

Sentence 1: Say your name and your company name.

Sentence 2: State in one sentence exactly what you do, in language that's relevant and compelling to the person who hears it. Sometimes we have certain phrases and certain words that mean something, but then if you switch the order, all of a sudden it's very powerful. Play with those words until you have a message that will matter to the person who hears it. It's not always what describes your business best, but it is what's going to get you through the door. Nothing else matters.

Sentence 3: Your expertise and credibility — this is your sentence number three. Why is it that what you do is so impactful and incredible for the people who hire you? Why do they hire you? Why do the clients say yes to your services? That's usually the basis of your statement of expertise and credibility.

Sentence 4: State why a meeting would be a benefit to the decision maker. Let's make it easy for that person to understand why a meeting would be useful.

Sentence 5: Give your phone number with spaces in between the digits.

Sentence 6: Provide the close.

A sample message: *"Hi Bill, this is Pat Iyer and I'm calling with Med League. We supply well-qualified nursing experts to help plaintiff attorneys settle their cases. I'd like to get some time on your calendar to talk about how we might be able to do the same for you. If you could call me, I'm at XXX-XXX-XXXX. I'm looking forward to speaking with you soon."*

That's an example of a voicemail message we would leave. It's friendly; it's conversational; it's impactful. There's a statement of expertise and credibility there and this is what will make a difference. We already know that content and delivery is what's going to hit your target.

Here is another format for a voice mail and some strategies from Colleen Stanley, who shared them on a National Speakers Association CD, for getting your prospect's attention.

1. Introduce yourself. "Hi (name of prospect). I am with (name of your company.)"
2. Refer to some event or problem that makes them a good prospect for you. Perhaps something happened to make them in need of your services. You can obtain this information by being aware of industry trends, changes, regulations, mergers, the information on the company's website, or through your referral source. "XYZ regulation that goes into effect on (date) is creating the need to_."
3. If you have a name of a referral source that the prospect is likely to know, you can use this. "Mr. (name) suggested I call you to…"
4. Identify your value statement. This would encompass the benefits to your client of working with you. This may be your elevator speech. "I specialize in working with law firms like yours by helping them to (benefits of what you deliver)."
5. Add social proof. "We've helped (names of clients, if you are permitted to share this) in a similar situation to obtain these benefits (explain them). What they received was (specify)."
6. Conclude the call by identifying when you will call back and also leave your contact information.

When you do your business development calls, close your email, close your cell phone, close your door. Turn off everything that would be a distraction and keep your eyes on your prospect list and where you left off because having time live with a prospect is like valuable real estate and it doesn't come along very often. Look at all the work you did to get here to this very moment. You have to make the most of it. So make sure that you're focused and you know exactly what you're going to say.

Mailing Information Followed by Calls

Assemble your materials: a business card, a CV/resume that emphasizes your nursing knowledge and all of your years of nursing experience, and what you have done in the field.

Should you send out informational packets first, followed by a call within one to two weeks OR call potential clients first? There are two parts to that answer. Most typically you will place the phone call first. Leave one to two voice mails before starting to email. Your email follows up the voice mail and has a few sentences, a couple of bullets, and a close.

Don't send out a packet and then wait two weeks. If somebody asks for information, send it by email, which is really the quickest way to do this. People are expecting that these days. A couple of years ago the packets were still going out, now it's more email than anything else.

You can follow up within 24-48 hours of sending an email. But if somebody asks for information, you need to send it out by the end of that business day. A lot of people will wait on that. Don't wait because there's a continuity to business development. That person will remember asking for that packet or that email, and when the person gets it the next day or later on that day, he'll remember you. A day later you call to follow up.

Now when you do call to follow up, don't say "I'm just calling to follow up." Instead, say, "I'm calling to be sure you received the information you asked me to send and to set a time to come in and talk to you in more detail." Because remember what your objective is, it's to get in the door. So we want to keep the language consistent with what your objective is.

When You Reach a Law Firm Attorney

Let's say you reach the head of the firm. This person is responsible for finance, case management, and overseeing associates, and more. So when you call and you want to talk about something that has to do with getting your foot in the door, the attorney may be facing getting ready for a trial next week. How much time and attention do you think you're going to get from this big decision maker? Probably not much at that particular moment and you could, of course, understand why, because what you're calling to talk about is not half as important as what that person is dealing with right now.

But that doesn't mean that this person shouldn't know about you, because it's the decision maker's inherent responsibility to maximize the price value relationship for anything she buys on behalf of the firm. Your product or service is one of those things. But you may just have to wait a little bit to get this person's attention. Have that empathy when you call if somebody is knee-deep in something else and say, "You know what, I get it. You're busy, I've had days like that. How about I call you tomorrow?" It will do wonders for your relationship instead of forcing a conversation on somebody at a time when he's just not ready to say yes to you. That is not going to help your relationship with that person. So hang in there and wait a little bit; be empathetic.

If you get somebody on the phone and he's really rushed and speaking very quickly, it is a natural inclination to match the cadence of the other person's voice and for you to speak quickly too. Don't do that. Slow down. He says, "I can't talk to you right now!" You can say, "Wow...you sound really busy..." and sometimes he'll slow down and take a breath and say,

"You have no idea!" and then proceed to tell you everything he's busy with including what you can help him with. So slow down the cadence of your voice.

I used to ask attorneys, "Did I catch you in the middle of something?" Finally one attorney said to me "Pat, if I wasn't in the middle of something, I wouldn't be doing my job." So then I switched the question to, "Did I catch you at a good time?" and that has proven to be a much better question than the other one. Most times people will say, "I have a couple of minutes." People usually have pretty good behavior when they're at work. When you call them at home, it's a whole different story.

We would rather have two or three more touch points that are good ones for the decision maker before we get the meeting than to force the meeting on somebody who really isn't ready to say yes right now. When you finally get to that meeting, the whole relationship will start off in a much better way. Securing the meeting is the critical point of the call. Don't lose sight of this.

After all the effort you made to decide who to target, what to say, and how to overcome objections, be sure you ask for the meeting. Identify what your objective is in any communication touch point. As you're going back and forth with the person on the phone, make sure you keep an eye on what your objective is so that you get the outcome you're looking for.

When somebody answers the phone live, you can't read all those voicemail sentences that we just talked about because it's not conversational. Say your name and your company name, the one sentence of exactly what your company does and a question. Now this question should not be left up to chance. You should think about this ahead of time. If you are marketing expert witnesses, you might ask the attorney, "How important is it to you to work with well-qualified expert witnesses?" or "What keeps you up at night with regard to expert witnesses?" If you are marketing screening medical malpractice cases for merit, you might ask, "How important is case selection to you?" If you are marketing medical record chronologies and summaries, you might ask, "How easy is it for you to interpret medical records?"

What questions can you use that are going to be relevant and compelling? If you do reach someone live, what is the question that's right for you that's going to springboard that conversation? Think about all the different possible answers to the questions. And if you're not getting the answers you want, then you need to change your question.

Overcoming Objections

You get into a situation where you've identified the person you want to speak with; you have the message; you get her on the phone. You engage her in dialogue and now she gives you an objection, and you can't overcome it. The whole situation stops. You should try to anticipate the objections that you're going to get from your prospects. If you think through all the objections that you've gotten over time, you probably can identify about 95% of the objections that are going to come your way. And if you do that, you can also pre-think what those responses are going to be. Write down your two most difficult objections, the ones that really stop you in your tracks, make you hit a tree, and craft answers to them.

Here are some common ones:

- I have a paralegal. I don't need a nurse.
- I use my next-door neighbor, who is a doctor, to review my files.
- I have a nurse in house.
- I already use a legal nurse consultant.
- I am tremendously busy and cannot see you now. I don't do medical malpractice.

Once you've identified what the responses are, practice responding and don't forget to couple the answer to the objection with a request for a next step. For example, if somebody says, "Send me information," this could be a brush-off but sometimes it's not. You can get the appointment today without ever sending the information and it sounds something like this —

Attorney: "Send me information."

You: "I could do that but our information is very general in nature and I'd like to speak with you about how this applies to your work. How about let's put a time on the calendar for next week on Thursday at 10 and I'll bring the information with me. How does that work for you?"

You answered the objection and coupled it with a request for a next step. When you do that you're more likely to get a next step. Think about your decision maker. What is going to allow you to overcome that objection and get you to the next step? Practice your responses. Write down the objections and craft answers, and make sure that your answers are strong so that you don't get stuck.

Fitting in Cold Calls

How do you fit business development calls into your busy schedule? Schedule a time block that is just as firm as if you were at a meeting with a prospect. You would never cancel one of those. Consider your cold calling time at that same level of importance. Don't accept any interruptions.

When you are really busy, reduce the size of your prospect list. Let's say you only focus on the ten most important prospects to you. If you can't focus on the ten most important prospects, narrow it down to five and call your five most important prospects. And if you can't focus on your five, if you can't find time in your work week to call five people, rethink your desire to earn more money.

Track Your Progress

Create goals for how many attorneys you will contact each day. Track your progress. Whether you use a sophisticated system like salesforce.com or Goldmine or ACT!, or whether you're using an Excel spreadsheet, or whether you use a plain old piece of paper, the best tracking mechanism to use is the one you use consistently. Take diligent notes about everything your prospects tell you. Keep them in your tracking mechanism so that the next time you call someone you can look back on where you left off. Talk about that when you communicate with them next time, whether it's a phone call or an email.

At Med League, we implemented a system a couple of years ago for tracking the progress of inquiries. When an attorney contacted us, we filled out a prospect intake form and gather specific information and had a checklist on the back to make sure that we followed through on all the steps. We filed these forms, which were printed on orange paper to make them stand out, in a binder alphabetically by the attorney's last name. If the case came in, we took out the orange sheet and placed it in the case file folder.

We also maintained an inquiry binder. We used a loose-leaf binder with paper that were printed with a table. Its columns listed the name of the attorney, the name of the case, and the name of the expert that we referred, if that's the situation, and a column for the date.

Every week we pulled open that binder and make the follow-up calls and used our ACT! database to keep notes of what was said. We recorded if the attorney was going to use the expert, or if he said the case was on hold, or "speak to me again in a month." This system kept us very organized and visually on target in terms of who we needed to be calling each week. We used this system consistently.

Unscheduled Law Firm Visits: Cold Visits

I have described cold calls in this chapter. Now I will discuss cold visits. Consider walking into a law firm without an appointment. Fit this visit in between your own appointments. Use a giveaway you have created that has your name, website address and phone number on it. Go in and say, "I'd like to speak with a paralegal" because the paralegal has that attorney's ear. She may be able to get you in to see the attorney where the receptionist may not let you.

Not all firms have paralegals. You can ask to speak to the attorney or his legal assistant. Once you are past the receptionist's desk, tell them you have a gift for them. You wanted to let them know you were in town and would be happy to meet with them. Then try your best at that point, with that assistant, to get the one-on-one meeting with the attorney. Once you get the one-on-one attorney meeting, you have to focus on what it is that you can do for the firm.

Here is another approach to unscheduled visits. You may have three objectives when you walk into the office: a) leave your card and resume, b) introduce yourself and ask for an appointment to come back to meet with the attorney, or c) ask for the attorney's time while you are there. When you walk into a firm without an appointment, your main goal is to make sure you leave your business card and your résumé with the front office person, whether that is a paralegal or a secretary. Introduce yourself and ask for an appointment to come back.

Making that initial icebreaker with the front office, with the secretary or the paralegal is important and is a way to get your foot in the door. So the whole cold calling process need not be as scary if you know why you are going there, know what you are going to say when you get there, and are prepared if you do get to talk to the attorney. You will know your objective is to discuss the benefits of working with you.

If you have an opportunity to meet with the attorney, you may encounter the objections I listed earlier. You can turn this around by asking the attorney for his assistance since he is so well known in the area. What advice would he give you to get a business such as yours up and running? In the process, you will be explaining your services and subtly selling the advantages of working with a nurse in addition to paralegals. You will be explaining to him how you will help his colleagues, but you are really trying to convince him of why he would hire you. As a legal nurse consultant, you can do so many of the pieces that his paralegals were not doing, nor were they trained to do because they weren't nurses. As an added benefit, the attorney will be teaching you all the things that his paralegals are doing for him.

Getting Acquainted

Prospecting includes a getting-acquainted stage. Are you a good match for this prospect? At this time your goal is to learn as much as possible about your prospect because you may never have the opportunity to sell your services to that person again. You should also assess whether the person is a good match for your business. Communicating your competitive advantage begins in the getting-acquainted stage. This is when your prospect is looking at you and comparing you with the competition. Your goal at this stage is to show how you can satisfy the prospective client's needs better than your competitor.

Establishing Rapport
A comfortable connection with a prospect helps to make a sale. This communication extends even further to how you present yourself. Neurolinguistic programming theory emphasizes that people like others who are like them. This theory suggests that you should blend in and mirror (match their body actions) of your prospect.

Have you ever had the uncomfortable experience of being dressed differently than others at a gathering? If you're at a barbecue and everybody's wearing jeans, you should be wearing jeans. But if you're at a meeting where everybody's wearing a suit, you need to wear a suit. Your image needs to mirror your prospect. You cannot go wrong if you are professionally dressed when you walk into a law firm.

Look for areas of commonalities. As discussed earlier, research your prospect before meeting with him or her. LinkedIn, your prospect's firm website, and internet searches may yield a wealth of information about your prospect. When you integrate this knowledge into your getting acquainted stage, your prospect may be impressed that you took the time to learn about him.

When you've gathered the research, use that to establish rapport.

Communicating Credibility

There are a number of ways that you can establish your credibility. You communicate your level of professional expertise with all aspects of your branding: business card, letterhead, email address, website, and signature lines. Communicating your competitive advantage and expertise can be accomplished in subtle ways. You may refer to work you've accomplished with clients, your educational background, your publications, or other strengths that set you apart. Figure out what competitive advantage you have, and then make sure to bring that into the conversation.

Goals of Face-to-Face Meetings

Your goal is to make a sale. This requires a positive mindset. What you focus on is what you get more of. So if you want to focus on the idea of growing your business, that's what you're going to get. The people you consult with need your expertise. It's a matter of building the relationships and making the connections that are going to result in business.

The getting-acquainted stage focuses on determining if you and the prospect have a good fit. Ideally you can achieve a face-to-face meeting to explore the opportunity to help your prospect and convert her to a client. This stage helps you decide if you should close the sale. Here are some questions that help you reach that decision.

1. What does the prospect need? What prompted the client to contact you, if he or she initiated the contact? What is the client's urgent need? Some people refer to this as the "what keeps you awake at night?" question.

2. Does the prospect need what you have to offer? Are you the right person to deliver these services, or should you refer the prospect to another person? For example, your prospect may ask you to do a life care plan. This project requires specific training and should not be taken on by a legal nurse consultant who is not familiar with the responsibility. Instead, you may offer to locate a life care planner to assist the prospect, and then to focus on what else you can do to help.

3. Do you find that the prospect can communicate well with you, or are there barriers that will be difficult to overcome?

4. Do you get any strong negative signals from the prospect that would make you hesitate to consult with that person? Is the person negative or abrasive? For example, an attorney asked me to meet with his team to discuss my services. He slouched in the chair and told me that everyone wanted to get into his pocket. He dismissed a sample report I did as "sophomoric," although his associates assured me they thought it was very effective. He told me he would have sued a legal nurse consultant who gave him an ineffective expert but found out the LNC

had no insurance. When I left his office, I had a pounding headache. I talked to a few people whose judgment I trusted, and found out this attorney had a string of legal vendors who no longer wanted to work with him because of his mood swings and cash flow issues. I wrote him a polite letter stating I was too busy to take on his work, and I have steadfastly refused to market to him again.

5. Does the prospect have the resources to pay for your services?
6. Is the person you are talking to a decision maker who has the authority to approve of the purchase?

Your Sales Pitch

Create an informative and persuasive presentation. Take the time needed to craft your sales presentation and practice the delivery. Be prepared to answer the questions about why you should be selected as a consultant, and why retaining you now is in the prospect's best interest. Build your case and identify your strongest points. Point out the return on investment your prospect will receive by retaining you.

Terri Sjodin of **SjodinCommuncations.com** presented a workshop that I attended in which she identified the 9 biggest sales presentation mistakes:

1. Don't wing it. You must be prepared.
2. Don't be too informative versus persuasive. Your job is to sell.
3. Don't misuse the allotted time. Divide the key points of your talk into the amount of time you have to deliver your message.
4. Don't provide inadequate support for why the client should choose you.

5. Don't be boring. Your presentation should be worth listening to. Be brief, clear, and concise.
6. Don't rely too much on visual aids. If you use PowerPoint, it should be a visual aid and not the center of attention.
7. Don't use distracting gestures and body language such as chewing gum, twirling your hair, or clicking a pen. Keep the focus on your message, not on your gestures.
8. Don't wear inappropriate dress. Wear your best clothes for a sales presentation.
9. Don't fail to close the sale. Ask for the business.

Consider combining mailings with in-person meetings. Follow up an in-person meeting with a thank you card. You might create a card with the picture of the person on the front of the card. For example, if you had lunch with the person, you may ask the waitperson to take a picture of you two sitting at the booth at the restaurant. You could send a card afterwards with that picture on the front and a little voice bubble that might have something that is humorous or thought-provoking.

These cards are kept and remembered. People don't tend to throw away pictures. So they're going to keep that, which means that you are going to have top-of-mind influence on them because they're seeing your card all the time.

Sometimes pictures are not appropriate or you don't have pictures that are appropriate to use. The inside of the card could contain a heartfelt message. Members of a society that is very connected electronically may appreciate the personal touch.

Closing the Sale

You've located your prospect, communicated your competitive advantage, and presented your expertise. You have determined that you have the expertise to assist the prospect. Now it is time to close the sale. Here are some sample questions:

- Does what I have explained sound like something your law firm would need?
- Does this sound like something you would want?
- What would it take to move this proposal from a nice-to-have to a must-have?
- What would it take to put this in your language so you would understand what I am trying to offer here?
- How do I make my services more appealing or relevant?
- When might you want me to start? This is called an assumptive close. You can also gain additional insight into the prospect's thoughts based on what he does with his eyes once this question is posed. If he looks up and to the left, he may be recalling what might prevent the consultant from starting. If he looks up and to the right, he's more than likely contemplating when the consultant could start, or assessing what might occur in the near future that would prevent such action. The prospect's eye movement would have to be confirmed (meaning how he displays such gestures) prior to posing the question.

Contracts

You have followed up to get a decision on using your services. You learn that the prospect wants to close the sale and asks you for a contract. You will need a contract that defines the services you offer. Contracts should identify services that you provide and make the client aware of additional services that you offer.

There are various ways of calculating fees. All include a provision to cover out-of-pocket expenses. Look for examples of contracts by doing an Internet search using the term "consultingcontracts.pdf." You'll find samples that will give you some ideas.

Consider your overhead and all of the expenses associated with running a business. Do not join the race to the bottom of the hourly fee scale. Know the typical fees charged by the people in your area. If you are aiming for a lower-quality or a lower-priced service, that's one level of clients that you're going to attract. If you're focusing on boutique firms, or being at the top of your fee range, then that will dictate another type of pricing.

Your contract should specify the payment terms. Include in your contract any requirements for interest that will be charged for late payment and requirements for retainers. Provide a contract that covers what you discussed with the prospect, but also offer a few additional options that add to the value and the cost of the project. Your prospective client may not have thought of those additional services and could decide to upgrade the project.

Carefully proofread your contract. Make absolutely sure you are sending the final agreement, and not a draft.

Modify your contract based on your experiences. Every time you have a problem with an attorney who doesn't understand some aspect of working with you, plug that hole in your agreement so that you can avoid problems by being very explicit. Those clauses are all from the school of hard knocks.

After your prospect signs the contract, do something special to enhance the relationship. Be aware that buyer's remorse may set in. Your goal is to have the prospect feel good about the interaction and be eager to start working with you.

Know, Like, Trust, and Remember

People say that they do business with people they know, like, trust and remember. But if somebody knows, likes and trusts you, but she doesn't remember you when she's ready to hire you, then it doesn't really matter how much she knows, likes and trusts you. Building that relationship and staying in touch is very important for being hired. One of the keys is to establish yourself as a credible consultant and then keep your name in front of those individuals, all those prospective people that you want to work with, to continually be remembered. If you contact them today, they may not have a need for your services. A month from now maybe they will and if they've forgotten who you are, if you haven't left an impression and then stayed in touch, that makes a difference.

CHAPTER 5

Creating Your Professional Image

CHAPTER 5

Creating Your Professional Image

In today's competitive world, with so much emphasis being placed on how we present ourselves to potential clients, legal nurse consultants need to be well informed about what constitutes a professional image. In essence, this is about more than how you look. Your appearance is a reflection of your image and/or your brand.

Your Brand

I'll begin with branding. This term gets thrown around a lot. As defined by Entrepreneur.com, it is the marketing practice of creating a name, symbol, or design that identifies and most importantly differentiates a product from other products.

A simpler way to say it is that your brand is the promise you make to your customers or clients every time they do business with you. It is extremely important to start your business off on the right foot, consciously thinking about your brand.

Why is that important? It's the message that you are going to be giving to your clients every time they do business with you. It's what they are going to get and what they can expect.

It tells them who you are, what your service is going to be like, and how they can perceive you. It's all related to your brand.

If you do any general marketing research or specific research on branding, the subject of psychology will come up. Psychology is key to branding. For example, though I don't drink diet soda anymore, when I did, an image of the brand I drank gave me an emotional response. Maybe I'd get thirsty; maybe I'd anticipate the first swallow. I expected enjoyment.

That's a very simple example to illustrate the concept that branding creates an emotional landscape for the client or for the consumer. It builds familiarity, which creates a feeling of safety and comfort. My goal is that if I see the same type of clients and work with the same attorneys on a repeat basis, when they see my logo or my name they'll say, "I know that when I work with Pat, I am going to have exemplary service. It's going to be an impeccable presentation and reliable support."

Think of some familiar logos. A little alligator symbolizes Lacoste, the French sportswear company. This reptile is one of the top 10 logos in the world. Lacoste is a luxury brand. People who like wearing status symbols may want it.

Another example comes from the automotive industry. In Europe, cars like BMWs and Mercedes are considered ordinary. In the U.S., they are viewed as luxury cars. Same cars, different marketing.

Other very well-known logos include the Nike check mark, the Starbucks mermaid, and the red bull's eye that represents Target. Finally, who doesn't recognize the Golden Arches?

People have emotional connections to each of these images.

Because of this, when you think about building a brand, your image makes a good starting point. Ask yourself what image would best represent your business. High-end? Middle-of-the-road? Do you want to signal bargain prices? Cost is only one piece of the picture. You also want to think about presenting an image that suggests quality. If, for example, you were to write a report with lots of typos and strange typefaces, people might question how careful you were in your documentation for a case. They would doubt your attention to detail.

Ask yourself what you value most as a customer or client. When you're the client, when you're the consumer, what do you value? Most people will probably say customer service. When they remember their interactions with you, that's what's going to stand out as either a deal maker or a deal breaker. Consider all these factors and any others that are important to you as you define your style. Your style is critical because everything else you do will build on this primary decision.

Creating Your Brand

With so many legal nurse consultants vying for clients, how do you stand out? One of the ways is to clearly define your brand. First, you need to understand branding. Then you will learn how to use strategies to attract more *ideal* clients, not just more clients.

The brand perception is the sum of all points of contact. When that's consistent, when it's strong, people know what to expect and who to trust.

Branding is intangible, not just something you see but something you can feel. It's the underlying power of our buying decisions and the reason we reach for certain products. We make buying decisions every day from the food that we eat to the toothpaste that we use.

Pay attention to the feelings, the descriptions, and the expectations that you're creating for your clients. Your clients actually create your brand to some level; you just get it started. You influence the brand, but your clients are the ones that define it to some level when they start interacting with it. You learn from their feedback in terms of what they like and do not like about your services.

Your Brand Identity

Your logo is part of the brand. It's really a small aspect, but it's the piece of your brand that everybody can remember. Your logo symbolizes the services and products you offer and how they solve your audience's problem. Consider hiring a graphic artist to work with you to create your logo. Do not copy someone else's logo — that is stealing. Your logo should look good in color or black and white. You will need a high resolution version of it so you can make it as large or small as needed.

Brand identity is defined by your visual aspects. It's the letterhead and the website; it's everything visual that you can touch and feel and see. Your visual identity is the look and the feel of the marketing materials, the website, the images that are used, or the colors that are carried throughout the website. The logo is one piece of that.

Branding is consistent. Your logo, website, letterhead, and business cards should all be visually consistent. So no matter where or when a target member visits your website or touches your brand, they get a sense they've been there before; they've seen it before, and then they can trust that brand experience a lot quicker.

Branding is shaped by the perceptions of the audience. That's done through the characteristics we call brand attributes. It's also the emotional relatedness that we create. It's also the depth of that experience, or the brand promise. The fundamental idea behind having a brand is that everything a company does, everything it owns, and everything it produces should reflect the value of the business as a whole. That's the purpose of branding.

Our brand allows our audience to instantly comprehend the value. When you have the consistency and you have it clearly identified, the intention of your brand is identified. People can comprehend it much faster than when you don't have it. Especially in the legal nurse consulting industry you'll want to build immediate trust, credibility, knowledge, and experience. Branding helps you take that to a new level.

Logos

Your business name needs to be tied to your logo. Keep that logo simple, clean looking, and adaptable, meaning transferable. You should be able to use it as a header for your stationery or web site, in a business card, or as a stamp. In short, you should be able to use it anywhere. That's how it gets embedded into people's minds. As soon as people see that name, that logo, it's an instant connection.

What Branding is Not

A logo is not your brand, but it is an instrumental part of

it. Branding encompasses more than your logo. It's the logo design, the identity design along with all of your marketing materials and your website. All of those different aspects combine in making your ultimate brand.

Branding is not just your identity. Branding is much bigger than that; it is the overall perceived mental, emotional end value of your business and/or personal image.

Brand Consistency and Repeat Business

How do legal nurse consultants effortlessly earn repeat business? The answers to that question are doing a great job for your clients and having brand consistency. You need consistency because the point of that is, and why you get repeat business is, your clients know they can trust you. They expect the experience is going to be the same over and over and over. If they had a positive experience, they want to know that they can trust that and that it's going to happen again. That consistency is what convinces them that they can trust your services.

Brand loyalty is the same idea in a sense; more people are going to be loyal to that brand when they know they can trust it. They like it; they know it and it's going to keep them coming back.

Brand Standards

For example, suppose you supply nursing expert witnesses. Your clients expect them to perform at a certain level of performance. Some of the most disturbing messages that I had to deal with as the president of the company were from attorneys who were unhappy with our experts. It may have been that an expert that we supplied to the attorney was not functioning at the level we expected. The concern may have been that the expert was not returning calls, or the report wasn't prepared well, or it may have been missing something major in the analysis. Each one of our experts was representing our brand. They affected the ability of every other expert in the business to potentially get work in the future from one of our clients.

When you think of branding, it's not just you who represents the brand. It is the consultants that you may have, or employees or contractors that you work with. It's every experience that the client has with your company.

When you deliver consulting services, you want to make sure that your standards are consistent whether they're provided by you or someone else. You've got to live by those standards so your clients will come back. That's what's going to create the repeat business. It's when your clients can't trust your brand anymore that they move on to your competitor.

Branding builds the immediate trust, likeability and the confidence in a company. You've got to be clear on what those standards are and that you are consistently delivering on your brand promise. We cannot promise a quality product, and then submit something filled with typos or other errors.

Brand Touch Points

Touch points are everything you do, say, or visually display. It's everything your company does or your business does, or your employees do. It's all of the correspondence, all of the marketing vehicles that you provide your audience, all of the points at which you interact with your clients. That's what you've got to keep consistent in order to earn repeat business.

Your touch points could be your:

- website
- card
- letterhead
- voice mail message
- newsletter
- contract
- work product
- email signature line
- employees
- social media messages
- exhibiting banner
- brochures
- presentations
- signs
- packaging
- blog
- proposal
- videos

Stop and think through every single touch point you use. Is there anything that needs to be re-evaluated? Is there anything that's not quite aligned with your brand? Maybe you don't have your logo on it or it looks different for some reason. Evaluate all those areas and you'll find out whether or not it's being brand consistent and upholding brand standards.

The bottom line is the more clear you are on your brand promise and the experience, the more everybody experiences that truth at every touch point, the more they will come back. Make sure that every single thing, every touch point, every marketing item, all of it is in sync and that you're communicating that clearly through all of your communications and touch points as well.

Brand Equity

We build brand equity when we are consistent in how we interact with our clients during our touch points. It makes people feel good about working with you; it makes people trust you and creates the repeat business.

Understand the difference between the value of a known brand and an unknown brand. In a nutshell, consumers pay a lot more for a similar product if the brand is known versus an unknown brand. For example, think brand name versus generic when you buy over-the-counter medicines. When are you willing to pay more for the brand name?

You want your clients to stay with you because you have built up equity. They have had positive experiences with you as a legal nurse consultant; you don't want them to consider using another consultant.

Brand equity equals the value of the benefit received, less the price paid. So it's that difference that creates that equity in your brand and in your business. When your clients have a negative experience with you, that creates some negative brand equity. You can come back from it; you can bounce back from it. You can try to clean up the relationship, offer them a solution, but you may never regain that trust again.

Once you create your brand, once you discover it, once you have it in place, it's not something that you put to rest. It's something that you manage; it's something that you pay attention to. Your reputation as a legal nurse consultant and consulting firm is crucial. You can come up with a new campaign that might introduce your services to a different target audience, but you definitely have to manage it. It's a reputation that you have to maintain.

Pay attention to your touch points. Consider what you deliver as part of your brand, and work to continuously improve your services.

Dress for Success

The first thing that we need to do in creating our style is what you want your business to look like. It may begin with your personal appearance. Most of you in the legal nurse community are dealing with corporate America. This usually calls for a conservative and polished appearance. In terms of color, this means navy blue, black, and gray. Accessories are quiet and support the conservative theme.

In the East Coast, New York sets the standard. No-jeans policies are common in corporate atmospheres. People wear suits, and they're usually black. In California, you'll find a more casual clothing atmosphere. Regional variations mean that you need to take a careful look at the dress standards for your part of the country and follow them. The most important rule to remember is that when you are meeting a potential client, your first impression will be difficult to alter. Make it a good one.

Photographic Impressions

How you dress for your all-important headshot is equally

important. This is another first impression. Not only your clothing but the quality of your headshot are vitally important. A headshot is a photograph shot from the mid-breast or waist up. If you don't have one or if you're planning to get a new one, here are the suggestions professional photographers give to ensure that your session yields good headshots.

Bring three or four wardrobe choices. Make sure that all of these are cleaned and ironed for the best impression. The colors you choose should be neutral, i.e., gray, black, and navy. Avoid white and very bright colors for photographic reasons. Your hair and makeup should be as you normally wear them—or maybe better. If you do a good job at hair styling and makeup, do it yourself. However, for the best possible impression, you may want to use the hair and makeup person connected to the photographer you've chosen. Some will insist that you do so.

The process works this way: the photographer will usually take about a hundred or so images. This will be stored on a computer, so you'll usually be able to see your headshots immediately. The photographer will go over all the shots with you, and you can pick the ones you like best.

Normally in headshot sessions, 2 to 5 digital images get cropped for 8x10. Some photographers will adapt them for social media. Headshots should be updated every two years. You may be tempted to keep on using a headshot from your younger days, and you can get away with this in your personal use of social media, but this is not a good idea in a professional forum. Your headshot should resemble the person who's going to walk into a potential client's office.

Since headshot costs range from around $300 to $1,200, look around carefully. Get recommendations from colleagues if you like their headshots. Find out what services, such as styling, adaptation for social media, etc., are included in the price.

Using Your Images

Use them as widely as possible. The more recognizable and familiar you are, the more you're promoting your brand and your business. In this highly visual age, that's essential. You will need to use images to enhance the experience of your business. I always recommend that people use their headshots on business cards. The company **www.legalnursebusiness.com/ moo** does a very good job working with your image, using up to 10 different ones on your business cards for a fair price. The ones with rounded edges will not leave your potential clients with painful memories.

Use your headshot on your website, in print advertising, your brochures, marketing cards, or your counter cards. Make it a basic part of your promotion. Another good company for this is **www.legalnursebusiness.com/Vistaprint**. You can design your own promotional material. You can see the preview on the site, and their prices are excellent.

The Film Phenomenon

At this time, film is very much the coming trend in advertising and promotion. The availability of filming via a cell phone has helped to boost this development. Having videos on your website and a YouTube channel, or a presence on Vimeo make you highly visible and also accessible. You can use a 2-3 minute video to highlight who you are. You put a face to your name, say what services you offer, and how people can get in touch with you. If you choose to showcase more of your personality and more of your customer service, that's even better. It doesn't have to be fancy. Create a clean, crisp, simple message with great imagery.

Check out my site, **www.getbusinesswithvideo.com**. This describes a service I offer to provide videos for business owners. Most cost ranges are anywhere from $400 to $1,000 depending on what type of video you are actually going to end up with, how involved it is and etc. The most important aspect of a video you make is to be yourself. If you are part of the video, speak as if you were speaking to a potential client—because the chances are good that you will be doing exactly that.

Social Media

This can be a charged topic. Your age may have something to do with how much you love or hate it. You may be wary of its ability to suck up huge amounts of your time. However, it's a necessity in today's electronic age.

Below, I'm briefly describing the social media that dominate at the time of this writing. Be aware that new platforms are constantly emerging and that the rules of play for any form of social media frequently change. Facebook, for example, often makes new rules, and they can shut down your account without much notice.

You can send out the most dazzling email messages in the world, but people check their social media more than they do their email. You need to be visible there. It's the fastest way to connect with the outside world, and that's where your clients are. Learn it, get on it, and make it work for you.

First and foremost is Facebook. Personally, you connect with friends from high school, or you catch up on what's going on, and you read interesting articles. Think about how many times you've been on Facebook and seen a random ad or read an article, and it turned you on to something else, or it's led you to a business. It can move and motivate your future clients in the same way.

It's essential to have a business Facebook page. In the background of Facebook where it says settings, notifications, etc., a business page can be a great advertising/marketing tool. You can look in the background and find out which of your posts has done super well. That lets you key in on what your visitors are keying in to.

You can also advertise and market cheaply on Facebook. You can boost your post for as little as $5 a day. You're also able to tweak those posts and those advertisements to a specific demographic. It's super cheap. There's a way for you to connect your Facebook to your website, and it also connects to what's known out there as lead pages, which are basically advertisements that capture emails for you of potential clients. The bottom line with Facebook is that you absolutely need a business Facebook page and then you need to study all of the great things that it can do for you.

LinkedIn is serious and business focused. I consider it a priority in terms of social media. People pay attention to it. It's also an important location for your headshot. Join groups that have attorney members, answer questions, be helpful and professional. Use LinkedIn to connect with your target market. Join my Linkedin group: LNC Marketing.

Whether it's Facebook or LinkedIn, be very careful about what kind of photographs get posted on your account. Your grandchild may be adorable, but your photograph of you hugging him shouldn't be shown as your icon on your Facebook business page. It's even more important on LinkedIn. Look professional.

I give Twitter mixed reviews. For a long time it seemed that no legal nurse consultants were active on Twitter, but lately I've noticed more. I'm reconsidering my involvement here. It's potentially a good place to post links to articles and blogs you've written. Remember that there's a 140 character limit. Being concise counts.

How can you use it as a legal nurse consultant? Put a great image up there because image sells. Make little advertisements into a JPEG file like a picture and tweet that. Tweet little messages and daily tips on how to win a case, new research mediums, how you can present the best face in court, or how to win over your attorney.

Google+ is another social media site. The most important reason to put your business on it is Search Engine Optimization, which is a fancy way of saying, "Get your site found on a search engine." The basic tool is utilizing keywords to direct people to your web site. Google actually has some pretty good information right on its site about how to use Google Analytics. This tool can help you pick a name for a book or a web site. It can show you popular search terms. I recommend that you get familiar with what it offers.

Next up is Instagram. While this form of social media works best for image-driven businesses, you can use it as a legal nurse consultant. Create little advertisements, helpful hints, little tidbit facts, or whatever it is that you want to get out there every day. Post them as pictures.

This is a good time to say that you don't need to despair because you think social media is all about images. Use your imagination to find ways to utilize social media. Don't sell Instagram short. It's very popular.

Yelp is like a big online Yellow Pages. While it's somewhat image driven, it can give a little blurb about your business. What makes it valuable is that your past clients will leave reviews and testimonials about your business.

Marketing

Here's where new entrepreneurs get seriously upset. They say, "I have to do marketing. I can't take it. I hate it. I can't sell myself." Get somebody else to do it for you. Ask for help from your closest friends. Let them do PR for you. They can also critique your business. Ask them to look at your blog, your website, and your print materials. I said your closest friends because these are the ones who will tell you the truth. Your business is too important for you to get deluded by false compliments. You need to know how the outside world looks at your presentation.

Utilize your colleagues as valuable resources. They may know what the hot topics are right now. They may have great web designers for you to utilize. They may know about great office space or who's got the best deal on printing materials or whatever. We're all working towards the same goal.

Past clients are your #1 resource. That is why your customer service needs to be impeccable. If you give me great service, you will have the most loyal human being on the planet. I will talk about you to anybody and everybody that I know.

Amongst your clientele, you need to find your evangelist, the person who has a lot of friends, a lot of business connections, and has usually a very loud voice either literally or figuratively. They know everybody, and everybody knows them. When they speak, people listen. They are going to be your best marketing tool. When you find your evangelist, take really good care of them.

Network, network, and network with other business owners. Look to women's groups, church groups and community groups in the county, in the city, in your neighborhood, wherever you go. Get out there and chat with your hair dresser, your gym people, your printers and your cleaners. Let these people help you help yourself. You never know where your next client is coming from.

Don't underestimate the lady at the cleaners because you don't know who she knows, and that's really the bottom line. People actually like to help. If they know that you're starting out a new business or you're trying to build a business, people want to help. I know I do when somebody tells me about something that they're passionate about and they want to be successful. If I can help them, I will.

Bundling Services
Create some cost-effective packages for your business that may include throwing something in for free. It doesn't have to be work. It could be a special report or a book. Be creative. Make sure you're showing value in every package. People like packages because too many choices can paralyze them.

The Competition

You're not the only legal nurse consultant around. So how do you view others? How about as individuals, each with their own style, personality, sensibilities, and expertise? Your potential client isn't looking for a machine that spews out information and data. He or she is looking for an individual that's compatible, with whom he or she can work comfortably and effectively.

Having an antagonistic attitude towards your so-called competition will not get you one client. Having a cooperative attitude towards your colleagues will get you a lot. That also means that if your colleague lands the client you wanted, don't get bitter. Don't blame them. That client was simply a better match for her. You're going to find the clients who match you.

Focus on delivering quality customer service and a quality you, because in the final analysis that's what people are really going to come back to you for more assistance.

CHAPTER 6

Attracting Your Prospects

CHAPTER 6

Attracting Your Prospects

The focus of this chapter is to help you learn how to refine your marketing materials so that you can effectively reach your target market. Your marketing materials may be brochures, letters, a website, or other written ways of reaching your target market/prospect.

Know Your Target Market/Ideal Customer

One of the most important things to remember as you focus on your marketing is to think about who you're writing for and what vehicle you are using to reach your market. You have a greater chance of fulfilling the purpose of your marketing if you think about your ideal customer. The more you know about that person, the better. What's really key is to think about how that prospect or client might respond to your message before you start writing.

The more you know about your reader, the better — the reader being the person who is looking at your brochure or your website. You have to understand your readers' beliefs, their fears, their insecurities, their needs, and their desires.

Nido Quebain, who is the chairman-emeritus of High Point University in North Carolina and also an articulate speaker, reminds us that, "Facts tell and emotions sell." It is really through emotions that we are able to touch the needs of our target market.

The individuals who talk about ideal clients in the marketing world suggest developing an avatar or a typical buyer of your services so that you know whom to target. There are many different types of attorneys and many attorney specialties in the world, but specific ones are drawn to the services of a legal nurse consultant because of the services that we offer to people.

The first piece is to think about the gender of the ideal client that you are looking for. The realities are that in the United States it still is true that most of the attorneys who are in senior positions are males. There are some women who are in power positions in law firms, but in general, it still is pretty much a male-dominated profession. That is changing because there are a lot of people coming through law school now who are females, but the older attorneys typically tend to be male. Also, the people who are in power positions in larger law firms tend to be older, in their 40s, 50s and 60s. That may not be the case for practitioners who are out on their own and may be in a single attorney law firm or have a partner.

It is important to identify the type of practice that you are looking for. Are you specifically interested in targeting personal injury attorneys, medical malpractice attorneys, worker's comp attorneys, or attorneys that handle criminal cases? I don't want to say criminal attorneys because that's a really bad phrase, so

I have to be careful about how I refer to that group.

In my experience, attorneys who handle family law are typically not the people who hire legal nurse consultants, although they may have medical records on some of their cases.

What Does That Client Need?

Secondly, think about what your ideal client needs. What specifically in their list of issues frustrates them? They might be able to turn these over to you so that you can handle that aspect of the case for them.

What is their pain? In the marketing world we talk about "pain."

What are the things that they find difficult to manage?

- Is it interpreting medical records?
- Is it trying to analyze handwriting?
- Is it finding a well-qualified expert?
- Is it knowing whether they should take a particular case?

What do they get frustrated about?

- Is it an electronic medical record vs. a handwritten one?
- Is it the hours that they spend trying to pour through the mountain of records that appears on their desk or is scattered around their office?

If you've been in an attorney's office, you might see accordion cases filled with medical records.

- What are their hopes?

- What are they most concerned with as they are building their practice?
- What do they want out of the way that they handle cases, and what stands in their way that is frustrating them?

Fears

Plaintiff attorneys fear:

- Making a bad decision on a case.
- Spending money unnecessarily.
- Hiring an ineffective witness.
- Being blindsided by information.

I had a conversation with a plaintiff attorney who was questioning a cancellation fee in a fee agreement. He said, "What if I don't have any control over the fact that a trial is cancelled at the last minute?" His message was, "I'm really fearful of being committed to pay a cancellation fee."

What are the fears of a defense attorney? These could include:

- Displeasing the insurance company that provides work.
- Getting hit with a large jury verdict.
- Hiring ineffective expert witnesses.
- Not seeing the holes in the case.

The more you understand the pain points, fears and needs of your ideal client, the more you can target your marketing.

Right and Left Brain Functions

Right and left brain functions influence how marketing messages are perceived. The left brain is the organized, methodical portion of the brain. Think of people working away in cubicles. The right side of the brain is associated with fun, creativity, music, and relaxing.

Think of right brain function as people having a good time - having fun. We all have both components in the way that we react to life, but some of us have more highly developed left or right sides of our brains.

If you think about "facts tell and emotions sell," you can see that the emotional part of the brain, or the right side of the brain, is the part that we're tapping into when we are marketing.

Motivators
You've heard of the seven deadly sins:

- Greed
- Fear
- Pride
- Lust
- Laziness
- Envy
- Vanity

These are motivators and emotions; some marketing is geared to help tap those deadly sins. From the standpoint of marketing to attorneys, it's a little difficult to think in terms of marketing to lust, for example, or envy or vanity or even greed. However, fear drives a lot of attorneys in their reactions, as discussed earlier.

When we think about marketing to emotions, these are ones that you might see more in mass media in terms of motivators. Look at ads that are directed to these motivators. There might be a luxury car ad, for example, that might appeal to the pride of the owner and that sense of status. Think of the attractive woman standing by the car, and you combine lust and vanity.

Motivators Useful for Legal Nurse Consultants

However, there are also some positive motivators which I believe we use more effectively, particularly as legal nurse consultants and as nurses.

- Honesty
- Sincerity
- Empathy
- Sympathy
- Flattery
- Integrity
- Common enemy

We pride ourselves on being honest and being forthright in working with attorneys. We have a code of ethics that directs us to be very forthright and not perform unethical actions.

As nurses, we genuinely want to help other people. In fact, sometimes that's our downfall because we get hooked into assisting an attorney, particularly at the last minute. I have made my share of these decisions that have come back to haunt me. An attorney calls at the last minute, needs something done. At times, I have rushed to help him, and then had trouble collecting money after performing the services.

I have learned to always get money in advance. It takes a number of times for this to happen before a legal nurse consultant realizes that, no matter how appealing it is to try to help an individual at the last minute, you have to be a wise business person in the process. We may feel empathy with the attorney but have to make good business decisions.

We may motivate the attorney through sympathy, showing that we care about the people that we assist and the needs of their clients. When you use flattery, it expresses your admiration of a client or of a case that the attorney is taking on. Integrity is always a sound business behavior that builds trust and credibility and helps the attorney realize that we are doing whatever we can, but we're not going to perform dishonest or unethical activities. The common enemy is a marketing strategy that some people use that may imply that others don't have your best interests in mind, but I do.

When we think about the rational (left side) part of the brain, once a decision is made, people need a rationale to convince themselves that they're making a good decision. When they think they've made a bad decision, they experience what is known as *buyer's remorse*. There are a numbers of ways that marketers address this issue. They may, at the conclusion of the sale, provide, for example, reinforcement of the wisdom of buying that particular product. Have you ever noticed how a sales clerk in a dress department will tell you what a good decision you made to buy that item?

When a legal nurse consultant is supplying an expert to an attorney, for example, the legal nurse consultant who is aware of buyer's remorse might say, "this expert is really skilled," or "we've had positive comments about the skills of this person." That helps the attorney feel reassured and more comfortable with the decision to hire an expert.

Websites

A website is the most important thing that you could possibly do for your business. This is how you speak to the world. It has to be representative of your work, and it needs to be current. It also needs to look professional. It's a very important first impression.

People spend an average of less than 30 seconds on a webpage. If it's taking too long to load, they're gone. If you're not sure this is true, think about what you do when you go to a web site. How long do you wait for it to load? In a similar vein, how long do you stay there when you can't figure out how to navigate it? Other people are like you.

If you're in a situation where time means more to you than money, hire someone. As with headshots, ask for recommendations, and be sure to look at the website of the recommender. Find out everything you're going to get for your money. Learn how available the web developer will be. Realize that you'll still be involved, i.e., you will have to spend some time coming up with ideas for changes and updates.

You will need a URL and hosting service for your website. I definitely suggest that you do your research, but some of the easy ones are Godaddy (my affiliate link) **http://x.co/patiyer**. I recommend Site5 for website hosting. This is my affiliate link: **http://www.site5.com/in.php?id=241125**. There are usually monthly charges for hosting your site, so do your research.

Search Engine Optimization
Search engine optimization is about driving people to your website utilizing keyword searches. If I go to Google, and I type in "Legal Nurse Consultant," a list of 20 LNCs comes up on my screen. They are ranked by popularity and/or the paying customers of Google. The most important thing for you to know is not to overuse your keywords. Google knows that people do this, and they'll kick you to the bottom of the list if you do. For more detailed information on Google rules, go to their site. You need to do this periodically because the rules are always changing.

What does your website have to look like? People tend to like websites with moving images. Scrolling sites have also become very popular. The entire site moves vertically when you move your mouse. This is called a responsive design.

Your name and logo should be prominent. Your bio page needs to be short, to the point, and professional. Your home page should also make clear what services you provide. Make sure that visitors can easily find your contact information.

What Goes On Your Site
People don't always agree on the subject of listing your prices. As a legal nurse consultant, you aren't doing retail sales unless you are also selling books, reports, and other fixed-price items. These, obviously, need to have prices listed. The controversy is between people who say, "Yes, prices help me screen my clients." Others argue that price shouldn't be the primary determining factor in a potential client's choice.

I fall into the second camp. If your client is going to come to you based on price alone, you may not be getting the best client. You might be getting one who either gives you a fight when the bill is submitted or is very slow in paying.

You might also gain clients who, if they had a discussion with you about the quality of your services, could decide that you offer more for the money. I recommend that you have a form that offers the visitor a chance to ask for more information from you. That way, you capture his or her email address.

It's very important for you to have testimonials from past clients on your site. Visitors will look for this evidence that you provide great service. You also need to have a blog.

Blogging

A blog is basically a web page where you communicate with your clients and visitors. You can relate events of your business, give out tips, and educate your audience. It must be updated on a regular basis, even though this can be a time-consuming activity. You may be thinking, "I have nothing to talk about," but you do. Bring up something from the past. Bring up a good or a bad client experience that you've had. (Be sure to disguise the details.) Say what you learned from it and what you could have done differently.

Write about something NEW — nothing speaks success like making yourself look like you are super busy. Put down anything that you are working on right now. Blog about it and make it sound fabulous.

BORROW something — have a colleague come in and be a guest speaker on your blog. Invite someone who can write on something that is current and related to your business. Give them a blog post opportunity. They'll love you for it and your clients will love you too. It keeps you relevant.

Something BLUE — this is not where you speak about how depressed you are because your business isn't where it should be. This is basically when you talk about something that is super personal and passionate to you. It's where you give voice to something and where you can speak from the heart. Check out *"Legal Nurse Consultant Marketing,"* the next book in this series, for 2 chapters devoted to websites and blogging.

The AIDA Formula

The attention, interest, desire and action formula is a classic formula that helps frame how we put together our marketing messages and website content, and it ensures that we're looking at each of the steps of that selling process.

Attention

The first is getting the attention of the reader: the attorney who is looking at a brochure, a letter, or a website.

In a crowded marketplace and with people who are bombarded with marketing messages and information, it's important to think about how you can quickly, in a matter of seconds, stop the reader and intrigue that person to read more. You might have nine seconds, if you're lucky, if somebody is looking at your materials before that person's going to make a decision about reading further. So grabbing the attention is critical.

Graphics
One of the ways to command attention is through graphics

and images. Think in terms of pictures that will capture somebody's attention. One of the things to keep in mind whenever you are using pictures on your website is to make sure you have the right to use those pictures and that you're not violating copyright.

You can get images by buying royalty-free discs and CD collections from various sources. You can buy single images from websites inexpensively. Just make sure you have purchased whatever you're using and that you're not going to run into any copyright issues.

Keywords

One of the keys in marketing is to think about the use of keywords. Keywords are phrases that are likely to be put into a search engine and will help bring up your website. In our field, *legal nurse consultant* would be a key word or a keyword phrase and *standards of care* would be another keyword phrase.

An attorney who is searching for legal nurse consultants or on the subject of standards of care is much more likely to end up on your website if those keywords are prominent. Ideally, they're in the first several sentences in the first paragraph that would come up on a search engine or on a page. When they're scattered through the page, they will draw attention and traffic to your site.

Headlines

Another element of marketing is to think in terms of headlines. Headlines draw your eye and make you want to read more. There are many types of headlines.

These can be on websites or emails; they can be in marketing letters that you're sending out.

One example is to ask a question. A question might be, "Have you ever wanted to. . ." or "What's the biggest problem that you have?" or "Did you know. . ." and fill in the rest of that question This is designed to get the attention of readers and make them want to read further to answer that question.

Another way to use headlines is to create a sense of urgency — get somebody to act now. We know that most people who are going to investigate a service are going to do it at the time they first discover it. If you're trying to sell something, you're much more likely to have a buyer at that moment than if the person puts your marketing material aside and says, "Oh I'll come back to that."

"Drop Everything and Read This Right Now" might be a headline. This is also called a *fear of loss* or a *scare* headline. Another type of headline is an incomplete thought. "I almost cried when I read this" is an incomplete thought or "I didn't think it could get worse." Now again some of these types of headlines might work well for you, and some of them you might look at and say, "No, no, no, I'm not sure I would use that kind of a headline." These examples are designed to stimulate your thoughts.

Another very common type of headline is one that stresses a benefit. You can get lots of ideas by looking at magazine covers. For example, *Seventeen Magazine* has a number of benefit headlines. You see, for example, "Look Prettier than Ever for Your First Day of School, "Your Perfect Jeans," "Total Dating Confidence." You can see how these headlines stress benefits.

Another example is this headline: "The Number 1 Move to a Cute Butt." In tiny letters underneath it says, "It hurts but it works." Suppose the cover reversed the order. In big blue letters it said, "It hurts but it works" and in tiny black letters it said, "Cute butt." You'd have an entirely different sense of that headline, and you might not read any further if the headline said, "It hurts but it works." No one wants to have pain, but if you're seventeen, you clearly want to have a cute butt.

Some other types of headlines include use of intrigue: asking a question that raises some thoughts in the mind of the prospect. An intriguing headline is, "Can you pass the prosperity test?" What's the prosperity test?

What does that mean? That may create some curiosity.

Consider a news headline. The weight loss industry in this country is a multimillion dollar industry. A news headline might be something like, "Amazing new medical breakthrough for fat loss."

Testimonial headlines are more along the lines of what we might be using in our marketing materials on our websites. For example, a testimonial headline might be "Jane Jones, Legal Nurse Consultant, was directly responsible for helping me to win the largest case of my career." You can imagine how that might cause an attorney to stop, read and try to figure out what was the case about and who is this person.

Interest

Once you grab somebody's attention, then you want to provoke some interest. These are examples of banner ads that we have provided on our websites and the websites of our affiliates that stress benefits and are supposed to grab people's interests. For example, I created called "Kick Start Your Business: How to Use Smart Strategies for Growth" (**www.legalnursebusiness.com**). I emphasized smart strategies for business growth. In a course I presented through **www.legalnursebusiness.com**, called "Polish Your Writing Skills" the focus in is on the benefits of impressing your clients.

Some other motivational triggers that get people's interest are ones that you commonly see and can apply to legal nurse consulting services. The focus is on the benefits for the reader. Think about how, as you're doing marketing, you can use these:

- Make money
- Save money
- Save time
- Work better
- Learn something
- Live longer
- Be comfortable
- Be loved
- Be popular
- Gain pleasure

How can you assist with making money or saving money? Certainly when we help plaintiff attorneys, we help them save money by avoiding cases without merit or with limited possibilities of success. Much of our work product is designed to save time for the attorney, to provide quick references, to organize materials so that the attorney can work better, or use us to learn something prior to taking a deposition of a medical professional, for example.

Some of the rest of these are a little bit harder to tie into the legal nurse consulting services. We know that many attorneys have stressful lives, and if we can help them reduce their stress, they can live longer, be more comfortable, and have better quality existences.

One of the keys to remember is that the focus of your marketing materials is on the reader. "You" is a much more interesting word to the reader than the word "I." The readers are primarily interested in themselves.

They're interested in their problems, their needs, their hopes, their fears, their dreams, and their aspirations. We spend 97% of the time thinking about ourselves and that gives you 3% of your attention for the world, for your friends, and other aspects of your life.

In *How to Win Friends & Influence People*, Dale Carnegie said everybody has a little invisible sign over their forehead that says "Make me feel special." The vast majority of your marketing materials should be focusing on your reader rather than on yourself and your skills and your background and your competence.

Words that Will Kill Interest
When you're putting together marketing materials there are some things that you should avoid doing.

Guff

The first of these is *guff,* a term you might not have heard of. Guff is very stiff, awkward, complex language, and includes the use of passive voice. It's pompous; it's uncomfortable. It has awkward, long sentences, and is very complex. The difficulty with guff is that it tends to lose the reader very quickly and causes the reader to turn off.

This is a sentence from a letter that I received from an attorney:

> *Following up ours of March 31st, a copy of which is annexed hereto, I still remain very interested in retaining the services of an expert witness.*

This is very awkward; you have to read this even a couple of times to figure out what the attorney is talking about.

> *Screening Medical Cases For Merit — I will document the departure from the established Standards of Care. Identify the mechanism, degree and extent of injury, extent of recovery, short term and long term prognosis, future healthcare needs, and evidence of pain and suffering and show the direct casual connection between the acts of negligence and the alleged damages.*

This is a statement from a legal nurse consultant's website. It is meant to identify some of the services that the legal nurse consultant provides, but what you see as you just look at this from a distance is that it's a whole maze of words. It is also incorrect in terms of grammar. She does say, "I will document the departure from the established standards of care." But the next sentence, which is one long sentence, should start with, "I will identify the mechanism. . . "The best way to handle this is to break it into several sentences.

I checked this sentence with the Flesch-Kincaid scale. This legal nurse consultant's paragraph has the reading complexity of about sixteen on the Flesch-Kincaid Scale, which is roughly equivalent to having a master's degree. It would be so much easier for the reader if it were broken down into smaller sentences, easier to digest and to follow.

Check your Help file to get directions to activate this feature in your word processor. The scale is roughly equivalent to grade level.

Fluff

Fluff is a type of language that is hyperbole. There's a lot of fluff in marketing. You can see grandiose claims. It is a type of language that has clichés in it. Fluff terms are "world class," "top quality," and "seamless transitions." The phrases that you see include things like "leading edge," "best of the breed," "state of the art," "user friendly," "uniquely qualified," and "robust." These are all clichés that are fluff. They don't really mean anything but they sound like they mean something.

> *One unique service we offer is the development and creation of multimedia court room presentations. These presentations are used during trials, arbitrations and/or mediations.*

Is this a *unique* legal nurse consulting service? There are many people who are involved in helping to present materials in the courtroom and have a considerable degree of skill in doing that. So what makes this unique? How is this person backing up her claim?

Here is a great example of fluff from a real estate ad:

Set upon 54+-/ acres of the original Clynmalira land patent of 1711, in the heart of Maryland's legendary hunt country, SPRINGMEADE MANOR is a testament to the most ennobling of human pursuits. It is a home, an estate, that bespeaks a reverence for bold vision, thoughtful collaboration, and undeniable élan. A creation of indisputable beauty befitting the glorious grounds upon which it sits SPRINGMEADE is both a sanctuary and a triumph.

You can see that the person who wrote this put in some fluff. Look at this sentence: "(This house) is a testament to the most ennobling of human pursuits." What is that? Is it hunting, is it making money, is it art? What is this human pursuit that is embodied in this house? The rest of this fluff statement is that it "bespeaks a reverence for bold vision, thoughtful collaboration and undeniable élan, a creation of indisputable beauty befitting the glorious grounds." It's all fluff. It's even really hard to grasp what this is all about.

Geek

Geek is very technical language that doesn't really take into account the reader. Nurses, particularly inexperienced legal nurse consultants, are guilty of using geek. They may be using phrases that are very clear to them but are not clear to the rest of the world. The problem with geek is that it slows down comprehension and is likely to turn off the attorney.

HOSPITAL STANDARDS OF CARE

ASSESSMENT:

1. Assess fetus in distress via continuous electronic fetal monitoring (EFM). Evaluate FMR tracing noting:

   a. uterine activity:

   1) tachysystole - hyperstimulation (>5 UC's in 10 minutes or closer that q 2 minutes)
   2) polysystole - coupling, ineffective labor pattern
   3) hypertonia - palpate for uterine relaxation following contraction
   4) absence of uterine tone - uterine rupture
   5) tetanic contractions > 90 seconds long or > 70 mmHg in strength (IVPC)

Here's an example from a website of a legal nurse consultant who was describing hospital standards of care. This individual used abbreviations that were not spelled out, such as FMR and UC's and IVPC. These medical terms are probably not going to be understandable to the majority of non-healthcare providers.

Differentiating Yourself

One of the key questions to ask yourself is, "How are you different from your competition?" Who is your competition in your area? How are you different? What is your unique advantage? I'm using the word *unique* deliberately. What is it about your company that makes you special? What are your actions that back up your uniqueness? Are you competing or differentiating yourself on price; is that your competitive advantage?

Here are some examples:

- a number of years of experience in business
- having a top-notch staff
- providing great customer support when there's a problem
- having a variety of services

Desire

The next element of this formula is creating desire. We create desire with proof. There are different types of proof that you can use in order to establish your claims. Validate your claims and stimulate the desire of other people to use your services.

You may increase desire with *facts*, such as your location, the number of years you have been in business or your services.

You may increase desire with *images*, such as before and after pictures or examples of demonstrative evidence.

You may increase desire by focusing on the risks of not using an LNC: costs and consequences of inaction, case studies, or negative experiences of non-clients.

Types of Proof

Social proof is a big component of sharing information that will reassure your client. Include testimonials on your site and in your marketing materials. Use video testimonials or audio testimonials from satisfied clients. The most credible testimonials consist of footage you obtain with a high-resolution pocket video camera or an iPhone.

Use a flip camera which costs a couple of hundred dollars. This is a very easy, lightweight camera to carry in your pocket and use at a conference, in the attorney's office, or wherever you are with your client. You capture a video testimonial right there, and then it gets loaded into the USB port in your camera. Then you can upload it to YouTube or edit it with any video editing software that you might have and create a testimonial very easily. The footage is of a satisfied attorney who is pleased with the work you did on a file. Make sure the testimonial is brief, to the point, and has good sound.

The second most credible testimonial is in written form, such as a letter or email you received from an attorney who praises your services. You may get an email from an attorney who says, "You did a great job. If it hadn't been for you, I don't know that I would have been able to make it to this figure on this case." Request permission to use this quote. Those testimonials show that someone appreciates your work, and it also makes you a trustworthy individual or company to work with.

The least credible testimonial does not use a name, or uses a first name only: "LNC, Inc. is a wonderful service. I highly recommend them, AH from Denver, Colorado." The Federal Trade Commission has focused on this type of testimonial and wants to be sure that people using testimonials are able to back up their claims. Those types of testimonials raise a lot of skepticism because some people have abused them and have frankly made up those testimonials. Never make up a testimonial.

Always strive to get permission to use the attorney's full name and location.

Getting Testimonials

How do you get testimonials? You ask. Get over your hesitation. I have found that attorneys are quite willing to share testimonials. After you've completed a case or a phase of the case, ask the client to give you a testimonial or fill out a feedback form.

Action

The last component of this formula is taking action; how do you get people to take action? Many legal nurse consultants provide guarantees to reduce the prospect's sense of risk. Overall, people do not cash in on their guarantees as often as you might expect. The guarantee might be something like.. "If you're not satisfied with your report, we will redo it at no charge." Very rarely do people actually take up somebody on that kind of a guarantee. However, they may instead never give you a second chance.

You can also anticipate the questions that somebody might have about your services and provide the answers in advance. What are the objections that a person might have? For example, "You're probably thinking, How much could this cost?'" That's a classic way of anticipating an objection.

In the marketing material that you prepare, have a clear and specific call to action. This tells the prospect exactly what you want them to do. Make it easy. "Call today, return a card, visit the website, fax back a form, request a free estimate, order online." Those are all very clear specific calls to action.

To sum it up, there is a very clear and easy outline to follow. Have a headline that stresses benefits. An emotional hook stresses features, including some social proof. End with a call to action.

Copy Writing Tips

When you are writing your marketing materials, a rule of thumb to follow is to do a brain dump first. Put down your ideas, then go back and refine your wording.

Remember that there are people who will scan, and there will be people who will read. The scanners are going to look for keywords, bulleted lists, and headers. The readers like to look for that longer content. Some will read every word. Use headlines for the people who read the first few words of the headline. They want to skip and scan and scroll. Remember to put your keywords at the beginning of sentences and in captions.

When people look at websites, they read in a roughly Z fashion. They go from top-left to right and then they go down to the bottom, and they again read from left to right. So this affects

- how you put elements on a page,
- how you would design information,
- here you would put photographs,
- the type of fonts that you use,
- the size of your text, and
- the lines or boxes or graphics or colors.

If you don't follow that Z pattern then your design can be confusing.

Another copywriting tip is to be very careful with how much bold you use. Words in all bold are harder to read. If you're using italics in large sections it can be difficult to read. We have been trained to think of underlining as a link. If you use blue text with underlining and it's not a link, it will confuse the reader. Be aware of those types of design elements and how they're interpreted by people.

Also, spell check and look to make sure you've got all the information about your company including how people can reach you.

Look at these examples of typos I found on legal nurse consulting sites:

Our services are helping attorney's every day.

Our reports clarify issues such as co-morbidity and failure to follow recommendations which can seriously effect case viability.

Pulling It All Together

In summary, what we've talked about is using the AIDA Formula. Get your reader's attention using visuals and headlines, ask a question, make a startling statement, and stimulate interest. Your focus should always be on the reader. Your readers are primarily interested in themselves, their needs, their problems, their fears, hopes, dreams, and goals. Marketing materials should make multiple use of the word "you" to focus in on the reader.

You want to create desire by stressing benefits and explaining what you can do to help the attorney. When you review websites of legal nurse consultants, you'll see overwhelmingly that many legal nurse consultants list their benefits secondarily. Primarily they stress their services. That's the opposite approach of following the AIDA Formula. You should first stress the benefits of working with you and then explain your services, not the other way around.

Finally, provide a call to action. Make it easy for your audience to know how to act. Call today, return the card, request a free estimate, order online, visit our website. Ask the reader of your website or your marketing materials to do something as a result of looking at your materials.

The effectiveness of your marketing determines the success of your business. Without clients, your finely developed skills will go to waste.

CHAPTER 7

Reaching Out to Attorneys

CHAPTER 7

Reaching Out to Attorneys

There are many places to meet potential clients. Meet them in person as well as online. Where's the best place to meet potential clients? Wherever the clients go is the best place to meet them (i.e. the events they attend, the organizations they belong to, etc). The answer to this question is going to vary depending on your ideal client. Do they go to meetings at the Chamber of Commerce once a month? Do they go to professional association meetings? Where do they meet? They meet somewhere. Use your investigative abilities to find your prospects.

Nurture Your Sphere of Influence

Your sphere of influence is the people that you have some connection with and even the people who *those* people have connections with. Who do you know who is an attorney? Who do you know who knows attorneys?

There are lots of other ways to connect with people we would call your sphere of influence. Much of your business within the next year will come from them. So the question becomes, "How are you staying in touch with those people?" Here are some ways to network:

You may prospect face-to-face or online though your website, Facebook, Twitter, or some of the other social media sites. Be cautious about overt selling on social media. Many people are turned off by sales pitches made on social media sites. *Network* through social media. Linkedin is useful for this purpose. You can do searches for the people you are trying to reach. If one of your primary connections is connected to that specific person, you can ask for an introduction. You can also send an inmail directly to that person if you have that level of membership in Linkedin. Learn more about using social media for marketing in Patricia Iyer, *Social Media for Legal Professionals* at www.legalnursebusiness.com.

Think about the benefits you offer an attorney. We've got to quit thinking about marketing LNC services and start thinking about how we're going to solve an issue or a problem for that attorney. You can't just go out there to sell your LNC business by talking about your services first.

If you say, "I can do a medical chronology," remember, so can their paralegal! You've got to define how you are different from a paralegal. You've got to think like an attorney. If you're sitting in that office every day, day in and day out, what would you be struggling with? Is it because you have electronic medical records that you cannot make heads or tails out of because you're not used to seeing them in that format? Is it a matter of locating an expert? Is it a matter of understanding a particular medical condition?

Some LNCs have gotten work by presenting a seminar for attorneys. You demonstrate your expertise, answer questions, and establish your credibility. Offer a one-hour program to get your foot in the door. Once you've got your foot in the door and are finished with the continuing legal education, the attorney may say, "I've got some questions for you. I have a case I want to discuss."

Your Competition

Successful companies seek effective ways to let the customer know that they're important and to stand out against the competition. Know your competition. In many fields the level of competition falls into two layers. One is the experienced business owner who has a client base that has been built up over the years. The other level is people who are trying to get into the field or maybe starting with a few clients and then building up. At that level there's competition in terms of quality; there's competition in terms of pricing.

There are some legal nurse consultants who underprice their services in order to get the work and therefore make it difficult for those individuals who charge what would be a more reasonable level for their services. Do not make this mistake. It is far harder to raise your prices to a reasonably competitive rate than it is to start at that rate. You devalue your worth by undercharging.

Here is a strategy that does not work. Do not call up your local competitors with established businesses, and say, "I want to be just like you. Please tell me everything you know." One naive legal nurse consultant used this approach with me last year when I met her at a conference. She sidled up to me, rubbed her shoulder against mine and said, "You're going to teach me everything you know so I can start my business in your backyard." In a word, "no." We have a business to protect, a client base that uses us, and strategies that we are not ready to share with local competitors.

Here is another strategy that does not work. Don't call up a local legal nurse consulting firm, pretend to be an attorney or paralegal, and ask for the LNC's fee structure. We can spot you. We know when you are faking it. We are protective of our information.

When a Prospect Calls

You may be approached by a potential client through fax, email, phone call, or an in-person conversation.

How do you handle this inquiry? The person may simply call for information, such as rates for services, or with a specific case in mind. Your intake system is critical because quite often it could be the first impression that a client is going to get of you or your company. Have a dedicated phone with a message on it that basically says who they're getting, so that they can leave a message. If you have young children, make sure they are trained to not answer that phone line.

Have a reliable answering machine attached to that line, or use your cell phone as your business line.

Consider a free service like Google Voice, which transcribes voice mail into emails. If you have somebody who answers your phone for you, it's important that they are well versed in understanding what services you provide and what services you don't provide.

Return phone calls within 24 hours. If you don't, the chance of losing that potential client is great. Let's assume you are currently working in another job, but you are trying to expand your practice in legal nursing. Consider this: what if I am at the hospital for 12 hours and I get a phone call? How do I get back to that person within 24 hours? One thing you can do is plan on returning that phone call during your lunch time or break. If you work a 7-to-7 shift you are going to need to call the attorney when he is there. You are better off trying to find a nice quiet spot, returning that phone call within the 24 hours, than waiting till you get a day off and then trying to return the call.

If you don't provide a service the attorney is inquiring about, establish yourself as a resource to at least send her to someplace else. Set her up with somebody you know who might be able to handle the case.

I recommend using an intake form that is customized to your needs. Record the essentials about the attorney, the case, the deadlines, and the services needed.

Include a checklist to show the steps you followed in response to the inquiry. Enter this information into your database. The intake system is a critical part of the business. Having a systematic way of recording that information saves a lot of trouble in the future when you are trying to figure out where you are on that particular inquiry.

If you develop systems at the beginning of your business, when you start having a lot of cases as your practice grows, you will have a sound foundation. When you start hiring staff, you will have a system that's already in place for them to follow.

When I first started my legal nurse consulting business, I bought a box of colored file folders. It had 7 colors in it. I assigned colors to different types of cases:

Red: A case I did as an expert witness for the plaintiff.

Blue: A case I did as an expert witness for the defense.

Pink: A case being completed by one of our expert witnesses for a plaintiff attorney.

Grey: A case being completed by one of our expert witnesses for a defense attorney.

Yellow: A non-expert witness case.

Purple: A case completed by one of our physician expert witnesses.

This simple system has saved several hours of work and aggravation. It makes finding a file folder much easier. Use a color-coding system that works for you.

Looking at Your Data

Always think in terms of what data you need. For example, what are the results of your marketing? When you get an inquiry about a new case, where did that referral come from? Was it an advertisement, another client, or a colleague? Your intake form should have a spot to fill in this information, and the data goes into your database.

What types of services are most requested? Are attorneys asking you to find experts, do research, create chronologies, or be an expert? This information will provide you with a sense of direction.

How much work are your clients giving you? Has that changed over the year? Let's say you were doing five cases a month for one attorney and all of sudden you realize, "Hey, nothing has been coming in from that firm." It's a signal that should stimulate you to ask why you are not getting more work. What happened? Did the attorney find another LNC? Did the firm close? Did the attorney leave? Or you might find out that there was a problem, and the attorney didn't say anything. She paid your bill, but you never got another case from her again. Tracking what's happening in your business is a critical way for you to look for trends.

Be Visible to Get Clients

Be active in your community and volunteer for responsibilities.

Consider visiting local schools and colleges and presenting what nursing has to offer. You may meet parents at various career days — parents who are attorneys, parents who work for insurance companies. This is another way you can get the word out about legal nurse consulting and about your business.

Be prepared to give your elevator speech. You need to be able to introduce yourself as a legal nurse consultant and add in one or two sentences about what it is you do. When you are face to face or talking over the phone to a prospect, you will have an opportunity to use your elevator speech. Cover your name, your business, and the benefits that you would provide to a client who is seeking to use your services. Your elevator speech should be direct, intriguing, and be stated in terms of the benefits you bring to your clients. Practice your speech until it naturally flows. The words and the phrasing of your elevator speech must be excellent. So wherever you go, have that presentation prepared, as well as your business card. Once you have worked out your speech, include the words in your promotional material. Those words are already in place, so make it easy for you and understandable for your clients.

In your community there are social or civic clubs, scouts and churches. They offer and are often looking for community speakers to come in and talk. This is a great way to start to learn how to present yourself and what you do. Present it to the eighth graders or to high school students who are looking into careers. They are a great audience because they are starving for the information, and it will help you to practice your presentation in order to then go out and speak to an attorney group or to an insurance company.

A "Lunch and Learn" helps to boost your practice. Ask for permission to go to an insurance company or law firm with basic sandwiches and set up in their conference room. Sometimes you may be able to get an audience to actually sit down and eat. Give a brief presentation. Or all you may have is time to deliver an elevator speech as various people came in to grab a sandwich. It is a way to actually make people aware that you exist and what it is you do.

Advertising

Advertising may be the least effective and most expensive way you can market your services. Face-to-face contact is the most effective means when you are talking to attorneys. Look for ways to conserve your dollars. Inexpensive ads that have a long shelf life are a good choice. Put together post cards or self mailers. Print in small quantities; you may want to change your materials after using them for awhile.

Look for creative giveaways that will also have a long shelf life. Don't invest in post it notes or candy with your name on the wrapper, for example. Attorneys will not hold onto those items. Look at the cost. While you can pay less per item by placing a larger order, think clearly about how long it may take for you to deplete your stock. Also consider the storage space. I know one LNC company that bought sports water bottles, which were big, bulky, and difficult to transport in quantity. It took forever for them to give away all the bottles.

Be careful about putting your business card on a magnet. I heard about a legal nurse consultant who put her business card on her magnet, and then the attorney put the magnet in her purse. It demagnetized the cell phone that was in the purse. And that legal nurse consultant got an unpleasant reputation for giving out magnets.

Strategies for Success

Set realistic growth goals. While you may hear that a legal nurse consultant can make $150 an hour, initially you may be working only 7 hours a month.

Recognize that the first case is the toughest one to get. You may feel like you are beating your head against the wall trying to get that first case. You know you could go out and actually do a wonderful job if you could just get started. I remember talking to an attorney who did not want to hire me because I had never testified as an expert witness. I told him that unless someone gave me a chance, I would never have the opportunity to testify. He did not hire me, but someone else did.

If you have never worked on a case but want to show a sample work product, take a case that you have read about. Create a scenario, and change the information up to make it fit the pattern of what you would prepare for an attorney. Save every actual case report you have done. Once it is settled or gone to trial, you can change names and use them as samples.

Starting a business can be all-consuming. It can be challenging to maintain a business atmosphere when you have children at home. You may need to hang a sign on your door that states your business hours. You are in your office during those hours and should not be interrupted. When you work at home, it is tempting to let the work day stretch until after dinner. It's very difficult to find down time, difficult to find time to go on vacation. You may go to a beautiful beach resort, and the phone's ringing constantly, and you can't just turn that off. But if you don't make your priorities, somebody's going to make them for you. If you need to carve out time out of the day for your family, put that on your calendar like you do everything else.

Don't put all your eggs in one basket. Even though business may be good and cases are coming in, you actually need to market when the case load is good so that you don't have as many of those bad times or down time. Don't wait until the down time to do the marketing or you'll be scrambling.

Make sure that you have savings and that you continue to invest in your own business as well — whether that's expanding your offers by obtaining another certification so that you can offer another service or investing in an exhibit booth. When the times are good, you need to be investing in your company and use that investment for your future marketing.

Know your strengths and find others to help you with your weaknesses. You can't and don't have to enjoy all aspects of running a business. Focus where your strengths are, where your passion is, on the things that come easily for you. You have to do those other things such as planning or doing the unpleasant portions of business until you can get to the point where you can hire staff or someone to help you.

You have to continue to be organized. Know that there are going to be setbacks. Prepare yourself for setbacks. Be prepared for attorneys who complain about your work product, invoice, or delivery time. Address their concerns, show you care, and improve.

Make yourself do something involving the business every day, even if it's a matter of doing some Internet research today to see what your competitors are doing. Or research www.Martindale.com to start a list of attorneys that you want to contact. Focus your effort every single day, even if it's only going to be for 15 minutes a day. Just make sure that every day you do something aimed at keeping your business on track. If you invest time into it, if you visualize it, if you can have a goal in mind for your business, you can achieve it. You really have to know what that business is going to look like and visualize that for yourself.

1. Read everything you can get your hands on about starting a business and marketing.
2. Spend some time developing new skills and relationships.
3. Visit web sites; not only of your competitors but also the attorneys that you want to target.
4. Network with everybody. Tell everybody you have a business and what it is that you do.

5. Make sure that you have your elevator speech down. Be able to, in just 60 seconds, explain to people what it is that you do in a way that they can share with someone else.

No matter what your background is, being a nurse is the most important part of it. You have many choices: expert witness work, subcontractor to another nurse, or consultant who does medical record organization and chronologies, medical research, or timelines. Find what you enjoy, what you are good at, what you are knowledgeable at, what you can get passionate about.

You can certainly specialize in those one or two areas.

Then see where your practice takes you. Let it develop. Listen to what your clients want. Provide excellent customer service. You will not build your business overnight, but persistence will be rewarded.

Chapter 8

Asking for Referrals

CHAPTER 8

Asking for Referrals

This chapter incorporates some of the things I've learned since starting my legal nurse consulting business in 1987. In January, 2015, after 28 years of running it, I sold this business. Now I help legal nurse consultants as a coach in assisting them to grow their businesses. See **www.LNCacademyinc.com**.

My focus here is on the value of referrals, i.e., asking people that you know or your clients to provide you with some names of people who may be interested in using your services. Such approaches are much more effective than asking people for business by making cold calls or sending out cold letters.

This chapter will cover how you can structure that conversation so that the people you're speaking to will be likely to assist you. I'll describe using a hook to capture people's attention so that they will want to listen to you. Once you get people who are interested in you, they are likely going to search on the internet for you and will check out your website. We'll go through specifically what you can do to keep them engaged once they come to your website, and we'll cover a lot more.

Who Do You Want as Your Clients?

There are really two parts to getting a client. The first part is getting in front of the right attorneys and the second part is everything that happens after that point. One of the key things that you have to do as a legal nurse consultant is to figure out who is your ideal client. Who are you trying to attract to your services?

Are You Referable?

In order for you to be somebody who can be referred to prospects or attorneys you have to be *referable*. In today's world, your reputation is even more important than ever before. Before attorneys had listservs, before they had easy access to emails, and before they talked to each other as readily and easily as they can now, things were different. If an attorney had a bad experience with a legal nurse consultant, maybe a few of that attorney's friends would hear about it. Today the attorney could describe what happened on a listserv, and it could be shared with 500 people in the click of a button.

You know that if you are going out to a restaurant, you might refer to a Yelp review of that place. You're checking out, and you're being checked out. You're concerned with how people are speaking about you, so you always have to be aware of your reputation and the importance of doing as thorough and good a job as you possibly can for each of your clients.

It's also important to know that in a networking environment or in an experience where you're asking somebody for a referral, your first position is to see what you can do to help that person. Instead of saying "Hey, help me! Help me," turn around and say "What are you interested in? What can I do for you?"

There is a law of influence called "reciprocity," which means that when we do nice things for other people, they in turn want to do nice things for us. They have a sense of obligation and want to help you when you've gone out of your way to help them.

Another important thing that builds your reputation is to consider what you need to do to stay on top of your game and to continue to learn.

- What new programs do you need to master?
- What changes in your business do you need to make?
- What do you need to learn to be more effective in analyzing medical records or marketing your services?

There is a continuum of changes. You can't rest on your laurels, and you can't stop learning. I continually listen to audio files when I'm driving. I'm always learning something new, taking new courses, reading, and going to websites. I'm always trying to build and improve on what I'm doing. It's very important for you to do that as a legal nurse consultant.

Another issue that affects your reputation and whether you are referable is your commitments to your clients. If you haven't already had the experience, you will someday have an attorney calling up on a Friday about 3:00 and saying "You know, I have this case and I kind of got behind on my deadlines. Do you think you can have it done by Monday?" If you think you can, you'll want to consider rush fees and the importance of using your opportunity for leverage, but don't over-commit and don't promise something that you can't do.

If an attorney comes to you with a case and says, "Will you

do this for me," you can subcontract it to a person if you don't have those skills, but don't make a commitment that you can't fulfill. This will affect how willing attorneys are to refer you to their colleagues.

Do you use integrity in your business practices? Using fair billing practices, for example, returning unused portions of retainers, helps to improve your reputation. I have gotten so much good will that I can't even quantify it from attorneys who have been amazed that when I was running my legal nurse consulting business, we would return unused portions of retainers. Sometimes they've encountered physicians who say, "This is my flat fee. I don't care whether it took me an hour to review it or 10 hours, but this is my fee, and I'm not returning anything left over."

One of my clients told me about a gastroenterologist who took a $10,000 retainer to appear in trial. At the last minute the trial was postponed, and this guy absolutely refused to return any portion of that retainer. The attorney told him, "Look, I know a lot of attorneys and I'm in a position to recommend you to a lot of people. Are you sure you won't return the money?" The doctor said, "Absolutely not." The attorney has never referred him or recommended him to anyone. This gentleman has lost a lot of potential business because of the position that he took.

In relation to raising your level and learning, always keep in mind what conferences you can attend and what people you might meet at those conferences. Get out of your four walls and recognize that this is all part of your development as a business person. Whatever legal nurse consulting training you had taught you some of the skills of analyzing cases, but there's a whole other level in terms of running a business that's really impossible to cover in a short course. Those are the things that make you successful, and you learn a lot by going to programs, meeting people, and asking questions.

Another thing that's very effective is to get a business coach. The **www.LNCAcademyinc.com** is my website for my coaching program. I think everyone who is serious about their business can get into a perspective of, "This is the way that I think I should be doing it" and not realize that there are many alternatives. You can learn a great deal from somebody who has created a successful legal nurse consulting business, as I have.

Referrals work. Compare them to a cold call, a cold letter, a cold office visit, or a drop-in at an attorney's office. A referral is a warm lead. You are already being recommended by somebody whom your prospect knows. There's already a level of credibility that's built into that recommendation.

People Want To Help

People have some myths about referrals that I want to go through with you.

One of them is that people won't share. In reality, attorneys are used to the whole concept of referrals. I don't know if you are aware that attorneys routinely make referrals to each other and they split the fees, particularly plaintiff attorneys. I don't think that defense attorneys have any financial role in giving referrals to each other because they're paid by insurance companies.

When a plaintiff attorney is soliciting cases, that attorney will work out a referral agreement with the other attorney and they will split the fees as the Model Rule 1.5(e) states. They agree in advance what percentage of the case work each of those attorneys will do. The client has to agree, and there has to be a reasonable total fee.

You may see advertisements in attorney websites, in newspapers or online that say "Send us your medical malpractice cases," for example. There's a very large plaintiff firm in the state in which I ran my business that advertises every week: "We are the experts in medical malpractice." They're gearing those advertisements to other attorneys who may have a client come into their office with a medical malpractice case. That attorney is not experienced in medical malpractice and wants to give that case to somebody who is an expert in that area. They work out a way to share the expenses, as well as the recovery if that case is settled or won in court.

It's important when you think about the sources of referrals to realize that literally anyone that you come in contact with can have a connection to an attorney, can know a personal injury attorney, or a medical malpractice attorney. Those sources could be friends, neighbors, people you sit next to on a plane, competitors, people in a coffee shop, your banker, your accountant, people in your health club, recreational groups, salespeople, alumni groups, people in your church, your family members, volunteer groups, prospects who have turned you down, your current clients, your former clients, trade associations, and vendors. It's really unlimited.

You never know who those people know, and that's the important thing. When you think about referral sources, don't look at the guy who's fixing your car and think "I'm not going to talk to him about what I do." He could have a brother who's a medical malpractice attorney. You don't know unless you talk to people and describe what you're looking for.

One of the people that I coached in the LNC Academy went to her dentist. She was speaking to the receptionist sitting behind the desk, catching up on what was new in my client's life. As she was describing her work, the receptionist said, "My brother is an attorney. He handles car accident cases. Do you get involved in those kinds of cases?" "Sure!" They were discussing this back and forth.

A man sitting in the waiting area of the dentist office waiting to be seen started listening to the conversation. He said, "Yeah, I know an attorney too." My client went in to get her teeth cleaned and came out with two leads just because she started talking about what she was doing in her business. Never prejudge who that person might know or where that conversation might lead.

Strategic Networking

There are some very defined strategies of networking groups that I want to go through, a couple of obvious ones and some that you might not have thought of.

The Bar Association may have networking events, educational programs, receptions, and organizational activities, and may welcome people who are not attorneys. It varies from place to place. I've had coaching clients who have had great success by going to horse races or networking events and meeting attorneys through Bar Association activities.

The Chamber of Commerce is another very important source of leads. The Chamber of Commerce is dedicated to the idea of helping local business people get ahead, and by local the emphasis is on your county. Every county in more populated areas typically has a Chamber of Commerce.

I went to a Chamber of Commerce luncheon one time in the city where I ran my business. When I walked in the door, I found out who was in charge of the event. I spoke to her and I said, "I'm here to meet an attorney. Do you have any members of your group who are attorneys?" She pointed out a woman in a red suit who was standing across the room.

I kept my eye on this woman, and I watched very carefully as she was heading toward the table to sit down for the luncheon. I grabbed the seat next to her. She sat down. I sat down. We started talking and then I began answering her questions about who I was and what my business did. She said, "Isn't it interesting that we're sitting right next to each other at this event? What a coincidence." I thought "Yep, a real coincidence." She ended up giving me some cases as a result of that event where we were sitting next to each other and getting to know each other.

You may not be familiar with The National Association of Women Business Owners. They are specifically designed to help women entrepreneurs in terms of creating wealth, promoting economic development, and building strategic alliances, coalitions and affiliations. They are all about helping women business owners improve their skills and get stronger.

Business Networking International is another group that is very specifically focused on helping business owners. They have a total of 3,200 chapters in the United States. They count their membership as of last year at 170,000 members, and they figure that they have passed about 6.6 million referrals, which have resulted in billions of dollars of business. They are very specifically dedicated to networking and making referrals.

Legal nurse consultants stand out as an unusual niche. Many people have not encountered legal nurse consultants. We're kind of a novelty. There's an interest in nurses in general as being perceived as helping, caring people.

Another opportunity to think about is attending an exhibit. You can either go to an exhibit as an exhibitor, or you can sign up usually at a discounted rate under a support staff rate, attend a conference, and use that opportunity to meet attorneys at breaks, people who are sitting next to you, or people who are in the hallways.

I devote two chapters to the topic of exhibiting in the next book in this series, *"Legal Nurse Consultant Marketing."* Get details at **www.legalnursebusiness.com**.

Exhibiting is a method of building a business that I found phenomenally successful in building my business. I first began exhibiting in about 1993, but in 1995 at my first time attending a national conference, which was held in New York City, I met an attorney who literally gave me so much business that he put my oldest son through an Ivy League education.

I went into his office to deliver a prize to him and looked at a set of medical records. This involved an approximately 3-month-old neonate who was in a neonatal intensive care unit and got an overdose of potassium chloride. He was supposed to get 3 mEq and the nurse gave this baby 30 mEq.

When I went in and looked at this record at the request of this brand new client, I recognized that the nurse should not have been giving potassium chloride by an IV push route. He asked "How do you know that?" I said, "Because I know that nurses who work in hospitals have to have a list of drugs that they can give by IV push, and I know that you can't give potassium chloride by IV push. That's used for lethal injections." He said that he had five doctors look at this case and none of them picked that up. I'm a nurse, and I saw that.

It turned out that the hospital did have a list of medications, and potassium chloride was not one of the ones that nurses were allowed to give by IV push. That changed the whole complexion of the case. From then on, we worked together closely for about the next 25 years.

Generally speaking, people have to start liking you in 10 seconds. Let's envision that you're in a networking event. You're talking to somebody about your business. You have to use a hook. You have to use something that's going to pull them in and get their attention.

You've heard that people have the average attention span of a goldfish — 7 seconds. They're sitting there listening to you. They want to quickly find out who you are quickly so that you can draw them in and intrigue them so that they are going to want to hear more.

Here are some examples of hooks.
- The attorney who says "I help clients win the game of jury lotto."
- The cosmetic dentist who says "We have a frequent smile program."

- The auto body company that says "We always meet by accident."
- Somebody who is in advertising sales could say "I help companies expose themselves and not get caught with their pants down."
- There are always the people in the hotel industry who say "I tuck people in at night."

The goal is to develop two or three different hooks and then test them out with people. When you get a positive reaction, you know that that's a keeper.

Now let's look at some specific LNC hooks.

"I'm your secret weapon in winning your case in mediation in the courtroom."

That could lead to somebody saying, "What secret weapon are we talking about and what does that mean?" That's a really good hook to consider.

"I'm a medical records detective."

"I can make your life a beach."

"I can show you where the bodies are buried in the medical record."

Sometimes these are difficult to come up with on the fly, so it may take a little bit of playing with it. Consider these and think about trying them out on people you know and asking for some reactions.

Referrals

People who purchase services, such as consulting services, may start with asking trusted colleagues for recommendations. If you are competent, competitive, and credible, you hope your clients will recommend you to their colleagues. Our clients can be excellent sources of referrals and word of mouth recommendations. This is the best kind of advertising — based on your performance, and at no cost to you.

Asking for Referrals

Some clients will naturally recommend you without your prodding. Others will do so after you plant the idea or ask for a referral. There are some strategies for obtaining referrals.

1. Send a subtle message to a prospect who calls you. Say, "If you are a referral to us, please let us know who to thank."
2. Encourage the clients who know, like, trust, and remember you to give you referrals. They have individuals in their sphere of influence who could use your services.
3. Give recommendations and referrals to your clients. If they are on LinkedIn, write a recommendation for your client. It is common practice to reciprocate.

Wording for Asking for Referrals

I know I sometimes feel awkward about saying, "Do you know anybody else who could use my services?" Is there any graceful way of asking for referrals from clients?

Here are some techniques.

1. "Who do you know I'd be a good fit for? Most of my

business comes from referrals."
2. "Referrals are always appreciated."
3. "The people who typically hire us are (describe your ideal client.) I have an important question. Could we brainstorm about who else would benefit from my skills?" Then ask the client to contact the prospect on your behalf to introduce you so the prospect will expect you to contact him or her.
4. A step up is to ask the person referring you to be part of a three-way call so that your referral can introduce you to the prospect.

The TRACK Method

What I'm going to share with you now is a very structured way of asking for a referral. I've used the abbreviation of TRACK to help you remember the steps. I'm going to go through each of the steps, and then I will share with you some examples of how these would sound in real life.

Tell
The first is to "**T**ell" the referral source that you are looking for referrals. In other words, tell them, "I build my business through recommendations, and I have found that referrals are a very useful way for me to get new business." So you're first explaining and sharing what this conversation is about.

Remind
The next step of this is to "**R**emind" people of the value or tell them about the results that you deliver. Say you're talking to an attorney whom you've worked for, and you want to ask that attorney for a referral. You may say something like "Remember what your business was like before we started

working together? You had medical records coming in all the time. They were piling up in your office ,and you didn't know what to do with them. Now you can call me. You can get a succinct summary of those medical records that helps you to come up with the appropriate legal strategies."

If you are not talking to a current client, you might explain in a few sentences or tell a story about the results that you've delivered for other people.

I've shared with you how I walked into the attorney's office in 1995 and immediately saw something that all of the physicians missed. That resulted in an uncontested liability and a check that was written for $7 million a couple of years later. That's a powerful story. It's a powerful set of facts that this child got a potassium chloride overdose, but it was key for the attorney to understand what happened medically, and I helped him in lots of different ways behind the scenes with that case.

Audience
The next piece is to be precise in describing your "**Audience**." Your ideal client is somebody who recognizes your services, needs what you have, and is capable of paying for it. This person is an attorney who handles cases with medical issues. Your contact could say, "Oh yeah, I know an attorney. He handles real estate closings. Can you help him?" "No, that's not my ideal client."

It's hard to imagine what medical issues might arise in a real estate closing, although I do know a story of a couple that went in to look at a house, and they fell through a hole in the floorboards into the basement. That was pretty dramatic, but it was a personal injury attorney who was telling me about the case and not a real estate attorney.

You're describing who are the kinds of attorneys that are your ideal customer, and you're telling the contact very specifically who you want to work with.

Contacts

The next step in this is to ask for a referral by using these words: "Who are one or two people you know who match the description of my audience?"

You pause and you wait. You remember from psychiatric nursing the importance of asking a question and then having silence rather than rushing in and trying to fill the silence. That gives your audience, your "contact," who's listening to you, the chance to think. "All right, who do I know who is a person who would fit this description of her ideal client?"

Let's suppose your contact says "I can think of somebody. I'm thinking about Bill Johnson." You say, "What about Bill Johnson made you think about him?" "He's an attorney who is in town. He's handling large personal injury cases. I know that he's very busy. I know that he doesn't have a nurse on staff. He's told me about how he sometimes brings medical records home and shows them to his next door neighbor who is an emergency room physician, but the doctor is not always available." You're getting some important information that helps fill out the picture of this individual, Bill Johnson.

Here's a very important next step that goes along with the context. It is that you ask for an introduction. There are only three acceptable ways for this introduction to be handled. One is to say "I'd like you to make a phone call to Bill Johnson and introduce me and let him know that I'll be speaking to him."

There's an email introduction, and there's a request for an in-person meeting. If you don't get one of those three steps, then it's a cold call. Your contact says "I'm sure he'll speak to you, just use my name." That's really no better than trying to get the gatekeeper in the law firm, and you know they're very good at screening those calls.

Instead, you request an introduction and say, "It would mean the world to me if you could introduce me to Bill Johnson."

Keep

You then "**K**eep" in touch by rewarding the person who's given you that referral, a handwritten note or a small gift. Let that contact know when you've gotten work from that prospect. You are reinforcing that wonderful behavior and encouraging that person to recommend other attorneys to you.

Remember the basic instructions of parents: say "please" and "thank you." Send thank-you gifts to your prospects and clients. Thank people who refer business to you. For example, at Med League we assembled gift packs. We included several useful items that we gave out when we exhibit at an attorney conference. We enclosed things like magnifying strips, pads of paper, pens, letter openers, coasters, devices that you can use to hold CDs, like 12 CDs in a zippered case. We have given out little toolkits that have little miniature screwdrivers in them. We assembled the gift packs; when they're put together they look more substantial than if it's just one or two items. You have great flexibility in terms of what you might want to include in such a gift pack.

We had a practice of sending out a handwritten thank-you card and gift to anyone who referred clients to us. I kept a stack of cards on my desk and handwrote a thank-you note that day, while I was thinking of it, before the information got buried by other priorities.

I always enclosed a business card. You can buy thank you notes or print up your own with your company name and contact information. Every once in a while someone called me with great enthusiasm and was thrilled with the package and appreciated being thanked.

When I ran my company, a small set of attorneys routinely, several times a year, shared our company's name with people they knew and we got lots of cases in as a result of word-of-mouth referrals.

There is plenty of work out there. It's a matter of building the relationships and staying in touch so you're remembered. When the time is right, you will get the business or the referral.

When you extend yourself to another, the relationships that you'll build will be amazing and it personally elevates you. When you start your day thinking about what you appreciate, what's good in your life, what's right in your life, it sets the tone for the whole day, and it's a really powerful tool.

Encourage your clients to do your marketing for you. A healthy business is in the process of these stages at all times. A base of repeat business and satisfied clients is supplemented by bringing new prospects into the business.

Example Script
So let me put this in action. I will give you two examples that show you what a conversation would sound like.

I'm talking to Barbara, my friend, and I'm talking about my coaching business.

I'm saying, "Barbara, since I sold my legal nurse consulting business, I'm coaching other legal nurse consultants to help them achieve the same kind of financial success that I did. I'm looking for referrals for legal nurse consultants who are serious about building their businesses. One of the LNCs I coached was able to leave her full-time job and now runs her own legal nurse consulting business full time. My ideal client is a legal nurse consultant who is emotionally and financially committed to growing an independent practice. Who are one or two people you know who would fit that profile?"

"You gave me the name of Gale Howard. What did I say that made you think of her? I would really appreciate it if you would introduce me to Gale. I'd love if you would call her now and explain who I am and that I will contact her. Thank you for giving me Gale's name. I'll let you know what happens when I speak with her."

Example Script
Here's another example. You're talking to a current client, an attorney. His name is Bill:

"Bill, I'm looking for referrals for attorneys who could use my services. My clients, including you, have told me that my medical record summaries give them a quick, easy way to get up to speed on the medical issues of their cases and this saves them enormous time. In fact, you remember that we talked about the fact that you wouldn't dream of taking a medical malpractice case without my assistance. I know that you've told me that you're settling about 90% of the cases that I have screened for you. My ideal client is in a small to mid-size firm who handles medical malpractice and personal injury cases. Who are one or two people that you know who would fit that profile?"

"You gave me the name of George Harris. What did I say that made you think of George? I would really appreciate it if you would introduce me to George. I will give you the text of an email to use and it will explain who I am and that I will contact him. I'll let you know what happens when I speak with George."

One of the keys in this is to keep in mind that you're not begging and you're not pleading. Begging comments are:

- You wouldn't happen to know anyone
- I was wondering
- I was hoping
- Could you possibly assist me

You have to be very firmly rooted in the value of your services and what you know. Now does this work? Yes.

In 1987, I did my first case as an expert witness involving a girl who fell in the bathroom of a hospital. Her glass IV bottle shattered. She fainted and cut her knees on the glass. Now that tells you how long ago that case occurred. If you've seen a glass IV bottle in a hospital recently, I would be surprised. When I finished that case the attorney, who was a defense attorney, was able to encourage the plaintiff attorney to drop the case.

What really happened, and this is the only time I've heard of this, was that after my report was written the plaintiff attorney called his client into his office. He said, "The defense has submitted a very good report. I don't think we're going to win." She said that she wanted to pursue it. He got out his checkbook and wrote her a check from his bank account to make her go away. She took the check and she left.

My client said that the case was dismissed with prejudice and I didn't even know what that meant. He told me that it meant that he could never re-file the case because of the fact that money was exchanged.

I said to my client, being completely naive and absolutely brand new, that I would really appreciate if he could give me the names of attorneys that I could approach about my services as an expert witness. "I'd like to have 10 names."

I'm not recommending that you ask somebody for 10 names. You will be more successful if you ask for 2 or 3 or even just one. I didn't know any better, and I asked him for 10 names, and he gave me 10 names. He gave me five defense attorneys and five plaintiff attorneys. I contacted every one of them. The second person I contacted had a case that was going to trial two months later and he needed an expert witness. The third person that I contacted asked me to go out to lunch with him. We discussed my services and he hired me. I think ultimately I got work from all of those attorneys, all 10 of them. All I had to do was ask.

What have you got to lose and then what could you potentially gain as a result of that?

More on Marketing

One of the myths about marketing is that just because I'm capable, I will succeed. The reality is that many legal nurse consultants have education, experience and expertise but are trying to get work and are struggling. They got all of that background, but they're having trouble getting cases in.

Mark LeBlanc, a past president of the National Speakers Association, is a small business coach. He says "The entrepreneurial graveyard is filled with business owners who had good products and services."

Understanding the way the healthcare system works is only the beginning of being a legal nurse consultant. It's the floor and not the ceiling of success. So if we put this all together, you have to know your ideal client, what that client needs, how to speak the client's language, and then demonstrate through your marketing materials and your messages that you have the knowledge that will help those clients.

Today somebody who's getting your name from a colleague may be checking you out before even picking up the phone to call you or to receive your call. The question is what are they going to find when they check you out.

Many legal nurse consultants have websites, but having a website is now the floor, not the ceiling. If you remember the movie, "Field of Dreams," this was a story about an Iowa corn farmer who heard voices. He interpreted those voices as telling him to build a baseball diamond in his fields. He did, and the Chicago White Sox came to his field.

This is Hollywood. Don't get trapped in the Field of Dreams thinking. That farmer who was hearing voices — you and I might call schizophrenic. If legal nurse consulting is a competitive marketplace with more nurses all the time coming into the field, you have to be willing to promote yourself, promote your website, continually look for ways to share your expertise, and create nurturing relationships with your clients.

It's a myth that you only need to have four pages on your website. This might have been true 10 years ago or maybe 8 years ago, but it's not true today. This approach is like the person with a bullhorn who's shouting "This is who I am. This is what I do. Call me." This approach does not encourage engagement. It doesn't encourage your prospect to speak with you. It doesn't give you an opportunity to find out who's been to your website so that you can stay in touch with that person.

It's also important to have a very professional looking website. There are sites where you can create a website in a night. They look often like they have been created in a night. You're building your professional reputation with your website and how it appears.

This is what your web site needs:

Describe the "Benefits" of working with you, in language that's directed to the attorney visitor. Look at your website. Print it out and use a yellow marker for every time you used the words I, me or we and a pink marker for every time you used the words you and your. I'll bet that you will find many of the pages on LNC websites speak about me, my, I and we and don't use the word you at all. Attorneys are looking for what are the benefits to them. How are you going to make their life easier?

The "About You" page is directed to the attorney. For example, "You are a busy plaintiff attorney who is faced every day with medical records that are coming in paper form and emailed to you. How do you make sense of all of that mountain of medical records?" You're directing the language on that page to the lawyer's pain points.

Because of the prevalence of video and the fact that many people prefer to learn by video, a "Welcome Video" is an important component to include on your website. It can be one or two minutes describing your services. You can be on camera. You can be a voice over. That's an important aspect of nurturing that relationship. See **www.getbusinesswithvideo.com** for details about video development that I provide.

Describing your "Services" certainly is important. A "Blog" is another way that you can connect with your audience. It's easy to do with a WordPress site. I'll be spending some more time talking about an "Opt-In." You've probably gone to websites where you can put in your name and email address to get a special report, download a video, or get some type of incentive so that you will give that information to the website owner. That person can stay in touch with you and connect with you in the future.

A "Contact Form" is another useful thing to have on a website. Because of the software that goes out and scrapes email addresses, I don't recommend that you put your email address on a website because you may find one day that you're selling Viagra through email instead of your legal nurse consultant services.

The "About Me" page is about you, the site owner, who you are — ideally with a picture — that describes your specific expertise. This is your opportunity to talk about your clinical background, your education, your certifications, and your special unique qualities that make you an appropriate person for that attorney to get to know.

You're demonstrating your expertise to your visitor through the information that you place on your website so that attorney is attracted to you and wants to do business with you and find out more. You demonstrate your expertise through that description of your background, through the opt-in offer that we'll talk about, and then your blog. This is where you're sharing with the attorney key information.

In *"Legal Nurse Consultant Marketing,"* the next book in this series, I devote a chapter to blogging. Get details at **www.legalnursebusiness.com.** Here, I'll describe it as a way for you to share information that may lead visitors to your website. Below is a quick example.

I wrote a blog once on a knee injury following a car accident. It was based on some research that I was asked to do about degenerative changes in a knee following the man's knee hitting a dashboard. The prospect was looking for a keyword related to knee injury, came to my blog, called me up and gave me a case because I had written a blog about the subject that was right in front of him. Literally the patient was in his office while he was talking to me.

The idea behind nurturing your prospect is first demonstrating your expertise. Secondly, you are nurturing your prospect by developing this relationship with your visitor so that individual knows you, likes you and trust you. Recognize that you have that medical background that will be effective in helping the attorney with cases.

Opting In

The "Opt-In" is rarely seen on legal nurse consultants' websites. I do see a lot of non-LNCs who offer a newsletter. These are the five words that really can kill your ability to attract people: "Sign up for my newsletter."

Individuals get a lot of emails. You might be horrified if you saw my inbox in one of my many email accounts. I have lots of messages, many of which are unread. You may have the same issue. People get lots of email, and they don't want a newsletter. What they want is something that's going to solve an immediate need.

The "Opt-In" is called a lead magnet. It's also called an ethical bribe and a freebie. It has several names, but when I refer to it now, it's the "Opt-In." This is really a secret weapon.

Your ideal opt-in form will have fields where individuals can fill in an email address, a first and a last name, the firm's name and then the type of law practice. This is a very helpful feature because by asking the attorney to fill in his or her background, your company is then about to direct information in the future to the specific interest of that attorney.

You might have a totally different subset of types of law firms that you're attracting or trying to attract. You might want to work with a worker's comp attorney or you might be focusing on criminal cases. That's really dependent upon your practice.

You might ask if the attorney is a plaintiff attorney or a defense attorney. Some attorneys do both. The bare minimum is to ask for an email address, a first name, and a last name. Offer a couple of things, and in this case there are a couple of reports that are available to attorneys that they can get just by filling in those fields.

The key is that in order to be able to take advantage of this, you have to have a website, or you have to be thinking about putting together a website. We've talked about the importance of having that know, like, and trust factor so that individuals will stay connected with you.

You want to offer something that's of value, something that they will perceive will be worth exchanging their name and their email address to get from you. There has to be a follow-up sequence. It's not enough to give the special report. You want to stay in touch with that attorney, so there has to be a system so that you can capture that name and address and then do regular follow-up. That's what attracts people so that they will share that information with you.

You may be thinking, "Well, how do I come up with an opt-in offer? How does this all fit together?"

A Program with You in Mind

I'm going to describe a system that has worked very well for me. I first started offering opt-in reports to attorneys probably in 2008. I built up quite an extensive list of attorneys who were interested in getting that opt-in offer. That enabled my company to stay in touch with them, to continue to send them helpful information, to tell them about our services, to develop that know, like, and trust relationship.

In order to assist you with this, I developed a five day coaching program to enable you to be able to create an irresistible opt-in offer. I worked with a woman from Houston named Brandi Spencer, who is a small business coach, to develop this program.

We structured it on the basis of five lessons. In this particular system, the POSST System, the first lesson is to focus on who is your perfect customer. We talked about the ideal client. I've talked with you about age, location, gender, type of practice, pain points and frustrations. The most important step in this system is to figure out who is your perfect customer.

The second piece of this coaching program is to work with you to develop an opt-in offer. This is the irresistible content, the valuable content, that you offer to the visitor to your website that will assist you in coming up with that, that you can offer to attorneys so that they will give you their name and email address and you can stay in touch with them. This program will work with you so that you will get a step-by-step guide for producing one type of an opt-in offer. I personally throughout this course will give you feedback on your content.

The third piece is to set up a system to capture email addresses. You've created a high-value opt-in offer. It's geared to your ideal customer, and you now need an automated system that will capture that email address. It's not going to work as your list grows to send out follow-up messages using your regular email system because those systems are trained to look for instances where people are sending out a large number of emails at one time. They will block those emails so that they will not reach the people on your list. I will recommend to you a simple-to-use system for your email marketing, or you might already have something that you're currently using.

This lesson will teach you how to create those lists of email addresses and tie them to your opt-in. If you're not a techie, don't worry because I will show you how to outsource the technical parts of this so that you won't get caught up in frustration with technology.

The fourth lesson is the sequence, those auto-responder messages that you send out to people. Auto-responder means you load them up so that if somebody signs up to be on your list at 8:00 at night you don't have to be sitting in front of your computer to send them their special report. You can set up those auto-responders to go out at anytime of the day or night in whatever sequence or frequency that you want and this course will show you about that.

Finally, how do you get traffic to your website, which is useful for getting people on your opt-in list but also to get eyeballs on your site from people who are your ideal client. How do you get attorneys to your website? We cover that as well in this course.

These are the pieces that you'll receive through the program, those five different modules that I've gone through. If you think you're going to be overwhelmed with information, don't worry. Each lesson's material is only four pages, so it's dense, highly targeted information in which I've distilled all the things that I have learned from having this system in place for seven years. You'll read each day's assignment. You'll complete it, and then I'll give you personal coaching to help you make the right choices.

You Will Receive Coaching from Me

When you join this program you will immediately receive all five lessons. You'll read through it. You'll have a chance to ask me a question. I will respond and then you'll do that assignment. I'll give you a response back within 24 hours. Once a day, Monday through Thursday, I go through my emails related to this coaching program and I will personally respond back to you so that you can make the critical decisions about that day's assignment. If I receive your question over the weekend, which is Friday, Saturday and Sunday, I'll answer it on Monday.

When you turn in your assignment, I will review it. I'll give you my personal feedback on it. Every one of those assignments has a clearly limited time frame, so you have anywhere between two to five days to accomplish each of those steps. Once I look at your assignment I'll give you that feedback, and then you'll see that progress. You'll get real results and you'll see real progress.

We then repeat that through steps two through five. After you receive my feedback, we're going to go through anything that needs to be adjusted, and then you'll have in place your opt-in offer that's designed for your ideal client. You'll know how to follow-up with that person and then how to drive traffic to your website.

We're going to focus on each of these pieces, including what's going to be irresistible content for an attorney. I'll teach you how to do one specific type of opt-in. There are probably dozens of things that you can offer, but for the sake of this coaching program we'll focus on creating a special report.

You'll have an email service that you've signed up for with an opt-in form that's on your website. We'll help you set up those follow-up messages and building the value so that you can keep connecting with the list of attorneys. You'll come away with some solid traffic generation ideas to get more people to your website.

You may be wondering, "Okay, I heard this description, and I understand the value," but believe it or not, this is not going to cost you a fortune. You'll find this offer here: **www.legalnursebusiness.com/optin**.

Learn How to Avoid Spamming
In addition to that five-module course, Brandi and I also collaborated on a special report called "Secrets of Creating and Promoting Opt-In Offers." We expanded on each of those pieces that are in the basic course to figure out exactly what your prospects want. We'll also show you 16 additional types of opt-in offers besides the special report. You'll then learn where I developed my graphics.

There are some very specific rules about spam. You'll learn what you can do and what you can't do. There are certainly some misunderstandings about this. I was talking to a man recently who said, "If I see email addresses on somebody's website, that means I can add them to my list." No, you can't. That's spam, and that can get you in trouble. We'll go through what you can do and what will get you in trouble.

I also will give you in this report some shortcuts that you can use for creating those auto-responder messages so that you got a head start in terms of the follow-up sequence. I'll also give you some additional ideas about driving traffic to your opt-in offer.

Learn by Videos

Finally, I know that some people have a desire to learn things by watching videos. You prefer to read or you may prefer to watch, so I've also found a video course that is just right on target for the information that's shared in this. It has nine videos. The whole course is a total of 50 minutes, so each video is no more than about 5 to 10 minutes long. There's an introduction that goes through how the course is set up. The Ladder gives you an overview of what you need to do to create an opt-in offer. There's a video that you will use to help you rapidly develop opt-in offers and then the fourth video covers different types of mediums or what is the type of opt-in offer that you should offer to people in exchange for their email address.

There's also very specific information on creating opt-in offers if you're selling a video course, eBooks, audio books or software. Probably the most important video is when you're selling services like we are as legal nurse consultants. How do you structure your opt-in to sell a service?

The lessons are delivered as PDFs. You don't need any software in order to go through this coaching program. You will have a deadline to complete the course. I put this deadline in because it's important that you take action on this. I have courses sitting on my computer that I purchased that I haven't opened up. I don't feel good about the fact that I spent the money but didn't go through the course. It makes me feel a little guilty, but I know that if I had realized that the course would disappear and I wouldn't be able to finish it, I would want to go through that course to make sure I completed it.

Although you have fa deadline to complete it, and it will not disappear off of your computer, your opportunity to ask me questions and feedback will disappear at the end of the time frame for completing it. You can certainly go through it at a different date if you wish, but I won't be available to give you that direct feedback beyond four weeks after you purchase it. You'll find this offer here: **www.legalnursebusiness.com/optin**.

CHAPTER 9

Managing Your Business

CHAPTER 9

Managing Your Business

Sometimes in our business, it seems that time is the commodity that's least available. What could you do if you had an additional month every year? Would you like to know how to get that?

The material in this chapter will teach you how.

How Do You Spend Your Day?
First, let's talk about your day. If your day is anything like mine, you get up, and you have a list of what you're going to get done.

If you're a sole entrepreneur as I am, maybe it goes something like this: You get into your email first thing because you have to see what's in there. You've got to make sure that your business is still running smoothly. You see that there's a request to review a case for an attorney. You know that you need to contact that person quickly so that you don't lose the case to another LNC.

You check your website and see it has a typo. It's something you haven't noticed before, so instead of asking a tech person to get in there and fix it, you log into the backend of your website to do a real quick fix of that one word.

Your day may start a little differently, but it's sure to include things that aren't on your list. Before you know it, your morning is gone. Maybe it's even late afternoon, and you know that everything you did was necessary. But you didn't get through your list of what you planned to get done.

You may be reading this and thinking, "I didn't finish that list that I was going to do yesterday," so now you move it to tomorrow's list. And you've got half of tomorrow filled up with the stuff that you were unable to get done today.

This doesn't happen only with your business. Maybe you know you need to set some goals and plans for your retirement, but you haven't gotten started yet. Something always comes up.

This problem will also affect your "off-duty" time. You might have your day off planned to do some fun stuff or get some errands done. You get up all ready for the day, and what happens? You might get a phone call from an attorney asking you to help her out. Maybe you have a nice relaxing evening planned, but one of your kids didn't get her school project finished. You have to stay up late with her to help to get it done, which now throws off your whole next day.

The bottom line is that life is full of time thieves. You know you need to learn how to handle them. As you think about how far you get behind in what you need to do, I know that getting your hands on that extra month every year is rapidly assuming even more importance.

Procrastination

There's always something else to do, maybe something easier than that chore that you keep putting off. Count on this: there's always something much more fun to do. Here's a quote from Christopher Parker that really fits with what I'm talking about.

"Procrastination is a lot like credit cards: it's a lot of fun until the bill comes in."

Sometimes our schedules don't work out and our lists don't get checked off because we're not focused. We're not staying on track, and maybe we're in high procrastination mode.

Goal Setting

What can you do? The first thing you need to do is to sit down and document your goals. They may be either business or personal goals. Here's another quote, from an unknown author.

"An unwritten goal is merely a wish."

Think about that: "An unwritten goal is merely a wish." Wishes are just ideas in the imagination. They are not necessarily things that are accomplished. By documenting your goals, they become more than just dreams and wishes.

- Do you want a new house?
- Do you want to travel?
- Do you want more money for your business?

Write down anything that comes to your mind. Write down any kind of strong dream that you have now or have had in the past. List those dreams because once you get them documented, they become goals. They become something that you can actually start working on. That's what's going to keep you focused and out of procrastination mode, having them written down.

Write Down Your Dreams

Do you have dreams that you would like to make come true? Once you know what those dreams are, go ahead and write down the most important ones, the ones you want to make real. Once you write them down, they become goals.

We'll focus now on your most important goal because it's most effective to work on one main goal at a time. What's going to keep you on track to accomplish them?

Think about this: Have you ever tried to put together a big party or a celebration without planning it all out?

- When and where you're going to have it?
- Who's going to be invited?
- What kind of decorations, food, or entertainment are needed?

If you've ever had to arrange something like this or ever watched from the sidelines when it was arranged, you know there are always a hundred big or little things to take care of, even with a list.

How in the world does it all get done and come together at just the right time?

I can remember organizing a party for my mother's eightieth birthday. The planning had a lot of elements. One of the most ambitious was to get comments and anecdotes from our relatives, including my mother's brother, nieces and nephews, and grandchildren. I also had plans to gather pictures and put all the material together into a souvenir booklet. This required lots of coordination, and it turned out to be a beautiful tribute to my mother.

The truth is that she deserves much of the credit for my success in organizing the birthday party for her. I know I was able to accomplish it—and many of the things I have to do in terms of running a business — from observing her skills in managing a complex and busy life. At one point, she was working part time as a nurse's aide, raising children, and going to college to get her degree. She graduated magna cum laude.

She was highly focused, and she never wasted time feeling sorry for herself and saying how hard her life was. If it had to get done, it got done. That didn't just apply to her. The kids had responsibilities, too. Household chores had to be done on time and done to a high standard of acceptability. Play time didn't happen until this was done. I don't think it's any accident that three of her four children ended up being entrepreneurs. They had been groomed in accountability.

Evaluating Your List

When you look at your list for the coming day, it's helpful to estimate how long each task will take. That will tell you whether you can get them all done. If you can't, prioritize ahead of time. Make clear decisions about what's most important. Use the same strategies when you break down the details of accomplishing your goals. Prioritize and plan out the necessary steps. If needed, break down the steps into smaller steps. Make this manageable.

How to Accomplish Your Goals

I'll set out an example. We'll say that someone wants to increase her salary so that she can set up a college fund for her grandchildren. That's a high-level goal.

The first thing you have to calculate is how old the grandchildren. How many years do you have to create and add to that college fund?

You're setting a time limit on it. What I'm giving you now are some examples of what are called "Smart Goals."

S — it's "Specific".

M — it's "Measurable".

The measurable is how much money are you going to put in and how often are you going to put it in so that you know that you're accomplishing that goal, that you're taking "Action Steps" working towards accomplishing that goal.

You're basically saying that you need to increase your salary.

- What are the things that you're going to do to increase your salary?
- Does that mean you're going to bring on more clients than you currently have and that will allow you to increase your salary?
- Are you going to take more money out of your business than you're currently taking out now for a salary?

Again, you need to figure that out. You see how I'm chopping down that big goal into smaller more measurable and manageable goals? You have two parts. One is to increase your salary and then the second part is to put money into a college fund for your grandchildren, but you have to do one before you can do the other. You have to get the money first.

This is how you want to start planning out the steps to accomplish that goal. You look at the goal as the high level and then you break it down into smaller, more manageable and measurable goals.

I gave you the "S" for "Specific." It's a general goal for money because you haven't said how much, but what you're trying to do is specific, and it's **m**easurable.

A — is "Achievable".

R — is that it's "Relevant." It's not floating out in the sky. You can grasp it; you can make it specific.

T — is the "Time."

That's why I said you know how old your grandchildren are and how long you have to be able to do this. However you acquire the money, you want to qualify it for yourself so that it is something measurable. You want to know that you're achieving that goal every time you put something into that account, and you can celebrate it. So there's our first celebration.

Here's another example. When I was at a National Speakers Association Conference in Las Vegas. I talked to a man who does business coaching. He came up with something very similar. He said that when you're establishing a goal, you should think of verb, noun and date such as "I will earn $110,000 a year by 2016." (My only correction for this is that I believe it is more effective to state this as if it's already happened, i.e., "It's 2016, and I've earned $110,000.") Remember the affirmations I described in Chapter 1?

Being Accountable

A friend of mine was a project manager in a corporation. She asked each person on the team to document their career goals for either within the company or for themselves personally. Some of them didn't have college degrees and wanted to achieve this goal. They didn't need them for their current position, but they did if they wanted to get promoted, either internally, or to a higher position in a different company.

After they documented their goals, she helped them lay out plans with action steps. They tracked everything on a regular basis. Everyone who documented their goals and followed their plans ended up with promotions either within the company, or they got higher positions in other companies. Some of those people tell her that they're still using those accountability skills. This is powerful evidence that they work.

- They had set their goals.
- They knew where they were headed.
- They were staying on track.

It's just another example of why documenting your goals, laying out that plan, and breaking it down into action steps really helps you to stay focused and on track. Document your goals. That's what's going to keep you focused.

We'll go back to the example that we had for the person who wants to have a college fund for her grandchildren.

Once you lay out the action steps that you'll take to increase your salary, you need to prioritize them because there might be 10 different things that you can do.

- Get more clients.
- Create services that you could sell to clients.

Find ways to bring in additional revenue, and once you lay out what those ways are, you need to list them in order of importance.

This method works for business and for personal goals. Creating the college fund for your grandchildren is a personal goal, but it's going to take effort through your business to accomplish that goal.

The easiest way to track your action steps is to document those and check each one off as it's completed. This is where celebration comes in. As you check off those action steps, deliberately stop and congratulate yourself for having completed them. No matter how small one may seem, each is a necessary element towards achieving your goal. You deserve congratulations for fulfilling them, and the more you fuel your sense of accomplishment, the more inspired you are to continue.

Documenting your goals keeps you focused, and having action steps keeps you out of procrastination mode. The methods you use to do this can be as simple as a pad of paper or as elaborate as a project application called Asana.com. You can also use Excel spreadsheets.

You'd identify

- The action

- When it needs to be done
- How long you think it would take you

Be sure to include a column for completion so that you can check it off and stop to celebrate getting it done. Don't make it complicated.

Track Your Results

Here's a question: Do you know what your numbers are, whether this is in regard to a business or a personal goal? Returning to the example of the woman who wants money for her grandchildren's college educations, if you were her, you'd ask yourself:

- How much do I need to increase my income?
- How much money am I going to save?
- How often will I save it?
- What's my savings goal?

You really need to have and track those numbers so that you can see that you're accomplishing things.

Here are some of the questions you could be asking yourself whether it's a business or personal goal:

- Do you know how much money comes into your household?
- How much goes out?
- How much money are you saving?

- How much money is needed for all that you are going to be doing? (You'll discover more tips about managing finances in Chapter 10.)

- How much time do you spend daily on things that you enjoy doing?

A lot of times we're focused on how much time we put into working on our businesses. We can forget about the importance of time spent in enjoyment doing a hobby, spending time with family and friends, or reading a good (non-business related) book.

You may be familiar with the law of attraction. Its basic principle is that what you give you attention to grows. If you worry more, you have more to worry about it. If you're fearful, you find more scary things. If you celebrate, you find more reasons for celebration.

If you don't document your goal, you're not focusing on it, so you're not going to accomplish it, i.e., you're not going to move closer to your goal. It's not going to become larger in your reality. If you get everything documented, and lay out that action plan, and start prioritizing by breaking it down in more detailed action steps, things are going to start happening for you.

I once listened to a talk by a psychologist who used this exact expression. He was talking about thinking of life as two columns. One is "problems," and one is "solutions." If you focus on the "problems," they get bigger and bigger. You get swamped with anxiety, depression and negativity. Ask yourself, "What's one step that I can use to address a problem?" You actually create a biological change in your brain. The neurotransmitters are different when you focus on solutions. This focus gets your adrenaline going. It gets your endorphins going. You have chemical reactions that move you towards the problem solving mode, the solutions. Helping you to achieve your goals is all about taking small steps. His expression was this:

"What you focus on expands!"

If you are focusing on problems, they dominate your thinking. If you focus on solutions, they will come to you. If you focus on celebration, you'll have more to celebrate.

I set revenue goals; I set task goals; I make long-term and short-term lists and check off the items. I celebrate. I highly recommend that you give this process a try. Are you familiar with this quote?

"Insanity is doing the same thing over and over and expecting different results."

Let's organize and run our businesses in sane ways.

Here's another piece of what makes this process work. You need an accountability coach. It could be a general coaching person or an actual business coach.

Please play close attention to the following: Don't use a friend as your accountability coach. Why? A coach is someone who tells you when you're off-track. A coach tells you the mistakes you're making. A coach tells you when you're procrastinating and not getting the job done. See **www.lncacademyinc.com** for details of a coaching program I provide to LNCs to help them achieve their dreams.

I'm not saying that a friend will never help you be accountable for yourself. A good friend will do that. On an ongoing basis, though, that's too much to ask of a friend. It becomes no longer a friendship, and friendship is too important to sacrifice.

If you don't want to or feel you can't afford to hire a coach trained to do this kind of work, consider a mastermind group. Either join one that's appropriate, or start one. Not all such groups are the same, but they can be organized so that people commit to goals and agree to hold themselves accountable for fulfilling them. Research this option if it appeals to you.

How To Get an Extra Month a Year

Now we're coming to the fulfillment of my promise at the beginning of this chapter. I'll begin with some facts. According to a CNBC News article, the average person loses 2.0 hours every single day by procrastinating and not doing the things that need to get done. The odds are that they don't have the all-important list I described. Two hours of procrastination every day equates to 31 days in a year. There's your extra month.

If you want that extra month, follow the steps that I've given you. Document your dreams, take the most important goal that you want to work on, lay out a plan, and break that down into action steps. As you accomplish them, check them off and celebrate. That will bring an end to procrastination. It's going to keep you focused and on track.

This is another instance in which a mastermind group can help you. It can be a place where you share your successes with others. This enlarges the spirit of celebration. And when we focus on something and enlarge it, what do we get? More. I will end the chapter with this thought: You have within yourself the power to make your dreams come true. Keep on making them happen, step by step, and don't forget to celebrate.

Your Business Plan

I have learned a number of ways in the past to fine-tune my strategic planning so that I can accomplish my goals more smoothly. This especially helps me with my business plan, the engine that delivers my goals to their desired destination.

I believe that one of the most important topics for any legal nurse consultant is establishing goals and a plan for your legal nurse consulting practice.

By business plan, I don't mean one that you're going to take to the bank, to angel investors, or to venture capitalist who are going to give you millions of dollars so you can build a big business. I'm talking about an "operating plan."

"What are you going to do?"

"Why are you going to do it?"

"When are you going to do it?"

"How are you going to do it?"

My first questions for you are: "Do you have a written business plan? Have you established those goals for this year or last year or ever?"

People I've coached have almost unanimously said, "No."

My goal is that by the time you finish this section of the chapter, you should have a much better idea of how to go about doing that. You could actually have written goals for your business within 24 hours if you follow the guidance here.

Urgent Versus Important

The first thing we're going to talk about is the difference between urgent and important. Steven Covey wrote about this in The 7 Habits of Highly Effective People. He outlined the differences between a squirrel and an owl.

The squirrel lives his life in a state of urgency. He always wonders where his next meal is coming from, and he forgets where he buried his nuts. On the other hand, the owl knows something that we and the squirrel don't: how to make choices between "urgent" and "important."

Steven Covey actually got this concept it from General Dwight Eisenhower, who called it "The Decision Hierarchy." It's a way of thinking about what's important and what's urgent and how to balance them.

Most of us can figure out how to do the things that are highly urgent and highly important. You don't need to read about goal setting to figure that out. Most of us also can also figure out not to prioritize things that are of really low urgency and low importance.

Our challenge is to balance things that seem immediately urgent but that don't compare in importance to things that seem to have low urgency but are really important for your business or your life.

The key challenge for your business is to recognize how your high urgency needs become easier to fulfill when you've devoted time and energy to the supposedly low-urgency needs.

Your Vision of Your Business
Please take a moment now and write down for yourself three or four words that describe your ideal LNC business.

"Is it going to be full-time?"

"Is it part-time?"

"Does it support your family?"

"Does it fund your retirement?"

"Does it send your kids to school?"

"For your own self-gratification, what do you really want?"

"How does your practice support the life that you want to live?"

Don't over think it. The best answers are those that arise spontaneously.

How Do You Know You are on Track?
Here's another question. For the coming year what three signals would tell you that you are on the right track? For example, do you need more revenue?

That's usually the first signal that people come up with. Or if you had more help, would that give you an indication that you were on the right track?

Do you need to change your client base? Do you need more of the ones who pay you a lot and pay on time and fewer of the ones that grump about paying and barely get around to it?

So write down some simple signals that would say, "Oh boy, if next year these three things had happened, I would be thrilled."

Some other answers might be a productive sense of accomplishment with the results being in the form of income. Someone else might be looking for a full-time legal nurse consulting practice and making her hospital job her hobby.

As we move through this subject, we'll see how we can make those signals a little more concrete and get them into your business.

Plan-Do-Check-Act

Another way to state this is what is known as Deming's "Plan-Do-Check-Act" process. You realize that your cash flow is way down, and it is because you have not been sending out invoices in a timely way. Many legal nurse consulting companies are challenged by the need to keep up with the flow of paper. How does a systematic quality improvement process apply to your legal nurse consulting firm?

The "Plan-Do-Study-Act" model can be used in many types of businesses. Let's apply it to invoicing in a legal nurse consulting business. Look at the problem from several angles, consistently asking why a certain process is in place or a certain thing happens. This is called drilling down to get to the root of the problem. For example, one explanation for late invoices is that your procedures for invoicing may be time consuming or convoluted. You may be inconsistent as to when you invoice — at stages during the case, monthly or at the end of the case. Are you busy turning out the work product instead of invoicing? Are you trying to juggle a part-time business and a full-time clinical role?

Step 1: Brainstorm in the planning stage. Determine your objective of doing a pilot test of a change in the procedure. For example, you may decide that you will take care of invoicing before any other work. State the objective of this test: having invoicing receive the highest priority. Make a prediction about what you think you'll find from your test.

Step 2: Do the test. Try it out on a small scale, and document problems or unexpected findings.

Step 3: Study the results. Look at the data, analyze it, and compare it to what you predicted you'd find. What did you learn from the test? Did you find the invoicing was being done in a timely manner? Did you find steps in your invoicing process that need to be eliminated or expanded?

Step 4: Act. Refine the change. Perhaps you'll decide to implement changes in your invoicing procedures. A change in software, procedures, or timing may be needed. Decide on a realistic plan for implementing the change, and plan the next test.

Careful examination of your processes will teach you what you need to change. Invoicing is the heart of your business. Don't neglect it. Figure out why you have roadblocks, remove them, and steam ahead.

Every day of every week we have to learn something new. This 21st Century information explosion is really hard to keep up with. You can't learn everything. Prioritize what you're going to learn.

The Balance Scorecard

"The Balance Scorecard" was developed by Robert Kaplan and David Norton at the Harvard Business School. It caused a sensation in the corporate world.

A balance links your long-term strategy, i.e., the important things, with your short-term actions, which are the things we need to get done urgently every day. It helps you to track your progress with "Leading Indicators."

There are four business processes connected to balanced scorecards. One is "Translating Your Vision into Action."

"Translating the Vision" is about clarifying and articulating it for yourself. If you have somebody who needs to be on-board with it, whether this is are a spouse, a business partner, or your employees, then having them form some consensus about what you're doing is very helpful.

"Business Planning" means setting our targets. We need to align the work that we're doing so that we're not working at cross purposes to ourselves. We have resources of time, energy, and money to allocate, and we need some milestones that tell us how far we are along the path.

The "Feedback and Learning" piece asks, "Is what I'm doing working?" That goes for your management style and communication style with your attorney clients and with your business partners. What do you need to learn?

"Communications and Linking" brings it all together. You may have people in your business with whom you need to communicate, especially when it comes to being able to translate your vision into language that people can understand and translating your plans into things that people can take action on. Learning and feedback help to assure that everyone is speaking the same language.

The "Four Perspectives" that Kaplan and Norton talk about for a "Balance Scorecard" are these four:

1. Financial
2. Customers
3. Business processes
4. Learning

Before I go any farther with that, I'm going to let you think about that for a minute. Most of the time when people start to think about business planning, they think about financial goals.

"I want to make $100,000."

"I want to have a $1,000,000 business."

"I want to. . ." (You can fill in the blank.)

The other things come as afterthoughts. This business planning methodology helps us to think about them all together without one being more important than the other. Have you given one of them priority in planning for your practice?

In webinars I've led, an average of 67% said they overlooked financial, 67% said processes, and 33% said learning and growth. No one overlooked their customers.

Keeping Things in Perspective

Here are a few more questions for you to consider.

- Why are you in business anyway?
- How does your business support the life that you want to live?
- What do you need to do that's new or different?
- What do you need to stop doing in order to move you in the direction that you really want?
- What motivates you to be in business anyway?

One key concept is "setting our strategies," which is the higher level thinking. Another is our "tactics," which is what are we actually going to do or ask somebody else to do from those "Four Perspectives."

We're going to look at "Leading" as well as "Lagging Indicators" (more of those later). We're going to "Measure and Track" our accomplishments, so that we don't have to wait until the end of the year and or get the bookkeeper in January 14th and find out whether we made a profit or not. We're going to think in terms of systems of how all this stuff fits together because neither the planning nor the execution stands alone.

The four perspectives are linked. You can actually start anywhere to think about this process.

- One is Waypoints — a term I like instead of objectives or goals because they might change.

- Measure — is how we're going to tell whether we're moving towards our "Waypoint."

The easiest way to think about that for the financial perspective is that your measure is dollars. "I want to make so many dollars per year," so measures are units.

- Target — is the number that I want to hit.

If we go back to the dollars per year measure, the "Target" is $500,000 a year. It's easy to say we think that way, but the reason we want to separate it in this "Balance Scorecard Planning" is that the measure would stay the same. This year it's still dollars per year. This year I might make $100,000, but next year I want to make $250,000. My measure won't change, but my target will.

- Actions are all the little plans and all those urgent things.

We make long-term and short-term "Action Plans" in order to get us to think. "I'm going to double my income next year because last year it was $100,000 and this year I want it to be $200,000." Then, what am I going to do?

Why is it important to do it this way? I think it's because most people say, "Oh, financial — I want to make $100,000 a year." "I've got to market to a lot of attorneys."

Maybe you do, or maybe you need to get more work from a small pool of attorneys. So you have to slow down here and think about what actions are really going to take you to hit this "Waypoint."

A lot of times people just jump right to the "Actions," and they don't think about what they're trying to do. They don't know if they're doing what they need to be doing.

How do we set these "Waypoints?" What are some of the "Waypoints" besides revenue that you might set for financial? We might have a "Sales Target" — more than just revenue.

We might have sales targets for a particular product. We might have a sales target for a particular region. We're going to add up all of our revenue, but we might have a specific target — a new type of customer, maybe a new attorney group, or maybe you want to target groups of attorney firms with more than 50 attorneys. Keep this in mind. In addition to the gross revenue, you may have the goal of getting those high-paying clients.

Here's an example from the customer's perspective: Maybe the customer is very happy with the things that you've been doing for him so far, but he would be interested in having some new services. So as you're thinking about your plan for this year, what new services might your customers want? Because it's the "Customer's Perspective" that counts, you might ask them what else they'd like to have or what they value most or what the competition is offering them.

Another "Customer Perspective" is about quality, and that could take a lot of forms. It might be your responsiveness to their phone calls. That's an urgent thing. It could be how much they value the expert testimony that you give them.

Next comes "Business Processes." One thing that's really big in the business world is on-time delivery. That could mean getting the reports you write to attorneys completed on time. It could be showing up to court on time or turning in a report early. The customer notices that even if he doesn't notice other aspects of your efficiency. You, however, have to plan for efficiency in all areas of your business.

Are there things that you need to do, systems to put in place in your business that would make it all much easier for you to do the things that you need to do? You can't be an expert witness if you're not an expert, so there's a lot of learning there.

One example of this is new software. Do you have a need to learn some new software this year? Do you need to learn more about how to conduct your business by hiring a business coach? I offer coaching through **www.LNCAcademyinc.com**. The people I work with quickly recognize how much they need to learn and benefit from working with me as an experienced LNC. Be open to the idea that you may need to learn a number of things.

Leading and Lagging Indicators
These refer to economic concepts. For example, the lack of businesses that need to recruit new executives is a leading indicator that the economy is tanking. At the same time the lack of available jobs is a lagging indicator, meaning that the economy is lagging behind expectations.

This, by the way, is one reason for you to check your after-tax profits more often than once, at the end of the year. You'll get a good sense of the indicators. You'll have an idea of what's working and what isn't.

These two leading indicators are really huge for small businesses:

- Cash flow — which means can you pay your bills on-time?

- On-time receipts — do your customers pay you frequently and on time enough so that you do have cash flow to pay your bills on time?

Many small businesses fail because they have receivables, but they haven't received them. Therefore they don't have enough cash to pay their bills, so therefore they crash. Obviously, this is a vital area for improvement.

Customer satisfaction is a leading indicator. Be sure to ask your customers if they're satisfied.

Ask:

- "How's it going?"
- "What could we do differently?"
- "What could I do better?"
- "Is there something you need that I haven't provided?"

That gives you a lot more real-time, short-term indication of what's going on than waiting around to see if your legal nurse consultant practice is the biggest one in Central Jersey or wherever you happen to be practicing.

The same thing goes for "In-house Business Processes": "How old are your receivables?"

That goes back up here to the on-time receipts, but this is a measure. A lot of times Chief Financial Officers measure the age of receivables. Very likely you do not have an employee called a chief financial officer. You are a one-person business

— in charge of marketing, doing the cases and creating the invoices. As your own chief financial officer, you should ask yourself,

"Why are these receivables so old? How come you did that work six months ago and you didn't get paid yet? Oh, you didn't invoice them until two months ago. What happened?"

Unfortunately that's not an isolated behavior among small business people. We did the work, and we think that people are going to pay us because they've always paid before. They're good people. They're attorneys, and they don't want to go to small claims court, but if you don't invoice them, they're not going to pay you.

Another issue is "Budget Overrun." That's a lagging indicator. Now I'm assuming that you have a budget, although lots of small business owners run their budget in the back of their heads, and they don't check it on a regular basis.

If you have a budget, it is a plan by definition. You look to see whether you're on target with your budget on a monthly or quarterly basis. Then you're a lot more likely to stay within that budget than you are if you just said, "Well, I know I'm over, but I'll make it up next quarter" or "I'll pay my taxes next quarter." This isn't a good plan.

"Am I up to the last minute preparing for my presentation or preparing to go to court?" You might be on time, but you could be highly stressed. If you have an idea that you need to be ready 48 hours before the court date, then you need to be prepared. When you achieve that goal on a regular basis, your stress levels will go down. You can also tell by your measurements that you're on a better track.

The last thing in "Learning and Growth" is learning computer programs or other things that we may need to do. Maintaining a database of your clients and your prospects is hugely important for small business owners. The biggest asset that most small business owners have is their prospect and client list. You hear about lists all the time in internet marketing. If you have people, including yourself, who are not proficient in keeping that database up-to-date and using it effectively, you are going to be in trouble. If you don't know how to keep your database current, you probably can't do your invoicing on time. Then you will have a cash flow issue.

Putting It All Together
Let's review these various measures.

"How much money do I make?"

"How satisfied are my customers?"

"How am I going to improve my business processes?"

"What do I need to learn?"

You may be the owner of your business, but you have help. Somebody else might be responsible for some of these aspects. We need to communicate with our people. If they have a set target and the action plans associated with them, you're much more likely to hit the target.

People who write down their goals and their plans have a much higher probability of reaching them or reaching close to them than people who do it mentally.

Here's a specific example from my business. A while back, we had to change all of our computers because Microsoft was going to stop supporting our computers' operating system. We had to invest a large amount of money in hardware, software and tech support. We had to do planning to make sure that the change over didn't affect our customers. We changed all the computers on Thursday night and then opened up for business on Friday to identify bugs so the tech support guys could work on the issues over the weekend.

We had in-house processes that we had to think of in terms of making sure all the software got loaded and that we had the appropriate licenses. Then we had a growth curve that would be involved in learning the new versions of the software programs that we used all the time.

We did this before it became a problem, i.e., before there was no more support for the operating system. Returning to the concepts in the earlier part of this chapter, this was performing a low-urgency function before it became high-urgency.

Examining Revenues

If you are in business, most likely you want to make more money. I explained "Gross Revenue." Another one is "Revenue Per Client."

Who are your most profitable clients? Identify your top 20% of your clients. Are they in the top 20% because they pay you the most, because you like working with them the most, or because they pay on time? What can you do to reward them?

Avoid rework and make your accounting easier. Let's say you want to not spend so much time on your accounting. How could you do that? Maybe you schedule one weekend day a month to work on that. Then, the rest of the time you don't have it hanging over your head.

Strategy versus Implementation

Here's a suggestion you can use to follow up on what I've explained so far. Take these four subjects: financial, customer, business and learning. Write down four things that you could do about "Financial Waypoints," four "Leading Measures," four of everything. Pick the best ones. If you just go with the first thing that you think of, take your thinking further. You don't want to be doing the same thing you did last year and expecting different results.

I can't promise you that you're going to double your sales, but I will promise you that you'll work more focused, more relaxed and more in tune with what really needs to happen for your business. You'll be working more towards what your customers need and easing your own business processes.

What you really want to do in order to survive is measure cash flow. If you want to succeed, you need to grow your sales and you need to become more profitable.

Chapter 10

Organizing Your Finances

CHAPTER 10

Organizing Your Finances

Business owners need to know many things: how to structure a business, manage one's mindset, set goals, and how to work on potentially delegating information or tasks to other people.

We also need to be familiar with very practical elements of our businesses. One of these key elements is money management. I introduced this subject in Chapter 9. This chapter takes you deeper into finances.

Over the course of my business experience, my husband has always managed the money part. This has made me realize how little I knew and how much I need to know about financial management. Since I sold my legal nurse consulting business, I have learned a great deal more about financial management, creating invoices, running profit and loss statements, and writing checks. I'm working with a coach now who works with me to create a budget for the year, which means projecting expenses and income.

Having learned how ignorant I was about the nuts and bolts of the finances involved in my business, I don't recommend completely turning over the financial management to a spouse or anyone else. I need to understand where the money is going, what's coming in, and types of deductions I'm entitled to take. You need this knowledge, too.

Smart money management will help you to both make and keep more money. You can best accomplish this by using simple and easy tools for managing and understanding your money.

These tools can also be used for your personal finances. You need to have both business and personal finances running smoothly in order to accomplish your goals. This is particularly important for people who run small businesses and who basically define themselves as entrepreneurs.

My intention here is to present simple and easy ways to track your money and set a budget. I'll give you some tips and tricks to understand your money, refine your financial goals, and use effective techniques to achieve them.

Keep It Simple

Let's identify and choose a simple and easy way to track your money and set budgets. How do we make it simple? The first step is to recognize that you may, like many people, freeze when you hear the words, "money," "taxes," "budgets," and related terms. If a method is simple and easy, you're more likely to follow it.

If I were to tell you to get a complicated accounting program, keep track of everything, and use double-entry systems with an accounting system, there's a good chance that you would be struck speechless and paralyzed. Once you recovered from shock, your first thought would be that you're totally incapable of, for example, even knowing what a double-entry system is.

Since all of us have different personalities, your personality has to play a part in it. Some people, especially if they have a scientific or mathematical bent, like complex forms like sophisticated Excel spreadsheets. Accounting software wouldn't work for them at all.

We also have to take into account that people have different styles when it comes to organization. Some of these relate to personal organization, such as where you put everything on your desk or how you arrange your receipts.

One suggestion is to have an inbox for all incoming receipts and paperwork. Once a week, you make a date to sit down and handle all of this. (One financial expert suggests that it's important to have a date with your money because money loves that kind of attention.)

You need a style of organization that suits your own style so that you'll do it. It has to be easy. There are lots of different methods of tracking.

Accounting Software

There are various versions of programs like QuickBooks. With QuickBooks Online, you can access your data online from anywhere. QuickBooks desktop is a little bit more comprehensive. You can share it with a different computer, with your accountant, or however you're using your data.

Some other accounting programs are Wave Accounting, Xero and Freshbooks. Wave is a free software program that allows you to do invoicing. Xero and Freshbooks both require a monthly subscription. In all of the above, you're the one who puts in the information. If you are at the point where your organizational skills and your personality say that accounting software makes much more sense for you, then that is a really good method of tracking for you.

Spreadsheets

Some spreadsheets are very simple. For example, you make a row at the top that says postage and make an entry every time you buy postage. A spreadsheet will do the addition for you, by category and by monthly expenses. You set it up in a way that best suits your needs. You can, of course, also use a spreadsheet for your personal expenses. It provides a very flexible way to keep track of both expenses and income.

Calendars

This may sound overly simple, but it can work, especially for entrepreneurs. Take the hypothetical example of a massage therapist. She writes down all her appointments in her calendar. She can total her income for each day in the appropriate square.

Tracking Expenses

You may be wondering how she keeps track of her expenses. I would suggest a different calendar for these, and I'd make the calendars different colors. This may seem obvious, but when this whole world of finance is threatening to us, there's no such thing as making it too simple.

An important expense that often gets overlooked is transportation. How far do you drive back and forth to your office? Do you drive to depositions? Trials?

By going to Google Maps or MapQuest, you can determine distances. Whether you note them in an accounting program, spreadsheet, or calendar, be sure to keep a record. This is a tax deduction, and the amount can add up very quickly. The same goes for keeping records of your car repairs. Because the travel allowance question can be very important to nurses who serve as expert witnesses, go to trade shows as exhibitors, or to conferences and seminars as part of continuing education, I'm spending a little time on this subject.

Bigger companies will tell their people they have, for instance, a $50 a day allowance to pay for their meals and such. The United States government has an allowance if you're gone away over a certain length of time from your primary place of business, and you're going there for a business purpose. If I'm exhibiting at a trade show, the government allows me a certain amount for travel, for hotels and for food.

This information is available on the IRS website. You'll need to prove that you did this travel and how long you stayed. Each state has a different rate.

You can get very effective use out of a day planner and an electronic calendar. You can use Google Calendars and/or one on your phone, whatever works best to help you keep track of things.

Pay special attention to situations where you're traveling out of town on business because these expenses can really add up. Wherever you note these expenses, be sure that you keep a detailed record.

Money or Revenue Logs

Your money log is where you're going to track your expenses. What did you spend your money on? This is vital information. The Revenue Log notes your income sources.

Take the example of the massage therapist. She could have revenue coming in from various sources. Let's say she teaches at a massage therapy school. She may also sell food supplements or massage products like oils and creams. When you have multiple income streams, you need to know how much each one is delivering.

For instance, I get income from seminars, private consulting, coaching, book sales, and some other things. I need to know how each area is performing. This helps me know whether some areas need more attention. It helps me allocate my time and money investments in terms of promotion.

From your point of view, what is the *least* important aspect of making your money tracking simple? Choose from these three: personality, type of organization, or type of industry.

If you chose type of industry as the least important aspect, that's correct. Personality and organization type, as I've been emphasizing in this chapter, are the key elements.

I realize that no matter how simply it's expressed, finances can be an intimidating subject, so I'm making a statement here that I hope will encourage you: Tracking your money is a key to success for any business or for any goal.

As I stated at the beginning of this chapter, a business coach will tell you that in order to reach your goals you have to know where you are. You have to know what your income is, and you have to know what your expenses are. To use the analogy of a road trip, you don't just put stuff in your car and say "Okay, we're going on vacation now," and start driving down the road with no destination in mind.

Did you pack clothes for the beach, or did you pack clothes for the mountains? Where are you going? And what if you decide that you're going to the beach, and you discover that you don't have any towels, bathing suits, or sunscreen?

It's the same with your finances. If you're going to have a goal, you have to know where you started from in order to create that map. You need to know what your financial resources are. Do the tracking.

However you do it, I recommend going back 30 to 45 days and tracking. I'm saying 45 days instead of 30 because there can be variations as to when you pay monthly bills. You might pay your rent on the first day of the month or on the last day of the month before. Weekends and holidays can have an effect on payment schedules.

This is probably the most important part. Find out where you are. Put down on that Money Log every single penny you spent and what you spent it on. Nothing is too small to note, whether it's a candy bar you bought on the way to a deposition or a newspaper. Write it down in your money log. If you're honest about your spending, you may be surprised to discover where your money goes.

Here's a very simple example. Suppose you rarely have breakfast at home. Instead, you stop off at a diner and have a doughnut and coffee. It costs you 4 or 5 dollars every day. That's $120 to $150 a month.

By being methodical and detailed about saving every receipt and logging them all into whatever system you're using, you'll discover where your money is going. Go back 30 to 45 days and track every penny. Gather every piece of paper and find out where your money is. Where are you spending your money? Have a day-by-day list.

You may be wondering how to handle quarterly payments, for example car insurance, which can be paid three or six months at a time. Take the amount and divide it by the correct number of months. If six months of car insurance is $600, put $100 down for each month.

Also look at the following:

- Bank statements
- Credit card statements
- Cash receipts

Make sure that you separate data into personal and business expenses because chances are, especially for sole entrepreneurs and some small business owners, that you mix them. Remember, if you don't treat your business like a business, the IRS doesn't have to, either. Also, when you're tracking everything make sure that you track money that your spouse or significant other and dependents are spending. You're attempting to determine where every penny is going.

After you've written everything down, and you know what you did the last 30 to 45 days, you have a good idea of what you're spending and what kind of adjustments you want to make.

What is your money, and where is your money? "What is your money" is more of a revenue question. If you look at the revenue log you're going to have days 1 through 30. Day 1 can be your husband's paycheck and the $5.67 interest that you got for the previous month on your bank account or a refund you got at Target. Whatever it is, it needs to go on that revenue tracking system.

One way you can get goal fulfillment involved in this process is to have the goal of filling every day with realized income. This makes the process more exciting and makes you more motivated.

Keep these things in mind:

Your system needs to be something that

- you'll use regularly, something that you'll definitely use
- something that's simple for you, and
- not time consuming.

I have heard people say that they spend two or three hours every day doing this. If you're one of them, please compare the method you use to the one described here. I'm sure you can find ways to streamline the process you're currently using. The bottom line is that two or three hours is much longer than it should take.

Budgets

Budgets enable us to be financially in charge of our businesses. There are different types.

1. Revenue and Sales Budgets

You're budgeting what money is coming in and by what means — for instance, products and services. I would recommend breaking that category down further. I, for example, have revenue coming in from book sales, coaching, webinars, and consultations. Even these categories can be further divided.

2. There are budgets that are strictly for the "Purchases of your Cost of Goods"

For instance, if you own a retail store, you need to know exactly what your products cost you, including shipping costs. For a legal nurse consulting business, you'd need to look at the cost of stationary, computer supplies, software, office amenities, etc.

3. Operating Expenses Budgets

What does it cost to keep your business running? This includes rent, payroll, insurance, advertising, and related items.

Tips and Tricks for Your Budgets

At this point, I'm narrowing things down with a sharper focus with regard to tracking your money. Make sure that you're flexible. You need to be able to handle the unexpected. That means making sure that you can be flexible with your budget and your money as you go along.

Review that your budget is consistent with your goals. For instance, you are attempting to grow your business by 100%. If you decide to increase your employee base from 0 to 10 overnight, your profit margin is going to suffer. While that's an exaggerated example, it emphasizes the importance of making your budget consistent with your goals.

There are certain types of goals and budgets that you need to set. Start with the short term, which is this year only. When it's running smoothly, advance to medium term which is 1 to 5 years, and then on to long term, i.e. 5+ years.

For the first year or two, you're probably going to be revising your budget quite a bit, so keep going with that short term focus until you get to the point where it is running smoothly. At this point, you may set the goal of having a million-dollar business. You may need to adjust the medium or long term budget to see how that can be accomplished.

Knowing where you are is key. Find out where you are. We'll be talking about adapting that.

You need to account for seasonality and trends. Although your business may be less prone to seasonal fluctuations, there may be periods when no one is going to court because of holidays or summer vacations. Attorneys tend to not send out much work from the middle of December to early January. These may be slower times in your business. If you've noticed such trends, adjust your budget to accommodate them. Make sure that during the slow periods, you have enough money put away to pay your bills.

Plan to evaluate the performance of your budget. At preset intervals, look at for its performance. Determine how you're doing, how well you're doing, and how well the system's doing.

Take into consideration employees and team members. Consider the value of your time and of your employees' time. People, yourself included, need to take time off for vacations, holidays, graduations, and other events. You need to schedule for this kind of down time. It's part of life, and it needs to be part of your budget.

In this vein, consider time that you want to spend with your family on a special trip or vacation. Your budget needs to allow for setting aside money for this kind of experience.

In terms of the value of your business time, review what you do personally. If you're spending a lot of time, for example, on accounting, does that mean your business has grown so much that you want to consider hiring an accountant? If you can find the money in your budget to do this, it's a very good idea. If you don't think you can find the money, approach the issue another way. How could you use the time you currently spend on accounting to bring more income into your business?

Cash Flow

Cash flow is an accounting and financial issue that legal nurse consultants face. We invoice attorneys for the work that we've performed for them, and then we wait for payment. Sometimes we wait and wait and wait for a payment. It can be delayed as much as a year or longer in some instances. If we work for the defense attorneys, the insurance companies have their own method of paying their bills. They may, for example, choose to pay their bill quarterly, and where they are in that cycle determines how long the legal nurse consultant has to wait for payment. Our financial performance can be caught up in this continual cycle of trying to collect.

One of the ways that I got around this in my business was to require retainers that have to be replenished once three-quarters of the retainer is used up. The attorney needs to send another retainer in order for the work to continue. This requirement dramatically improved the cycle of collections.

While I strongly recommend the retainer approach, some attorneys and some insurance companies don't want to adhere to that plan, which then keeps the company in a continual cycle of chasing money.

In cases like that, you need to do some revisions to your budget. If you know that an attorney is going to pay 60, 90 or even 120 days out or more, that makes it even more important to do the budget. If you know that you're doing the work in January and you're not going to get the money until May, on your budget you're actually taking that money you made in January and putting it as income in May.

However, you can't always count on that. Sometimes the plaintiff attorneys won't pay their bills until they settle a case and they are flush with money. They'll get caught up on all the cases in which they owed their vendors money. The unpredictability makes it very difficult for legal nurse consultants whose clients have that type of a cash flow issue. For example, in my state there were vacancies on the benches, and there was a political issue going on with our governor who wasn't putting judges on those benches. The plaintiff attorneys couldn't try cases, and therefore they didn't have the cash flow to be able to pay for cases that they already had in the pipeline. That set back a whole group of attorneys in our state for about a year.

Variables like that can be very challenging when you talk about trying to project revenue, and you've got fixed expenses and clients who are not paying their bills. You can threaten them with 1½% interest per month. Sometimes they pay the interest along with the invoice, and sometimes they leave off the interest and they pay the bill.

I know this issue isn't confined to legal nurse consulting. Cash flow is a prime challenge when you have a small business. If this is your sole source of income, then cash flow becomes very, very important. One of the better ways to handle that is to let reliability of payment help to govern which clients you'll work with. You'll choose not to take the work of some clients because they have histories of being poor payers.

Being able to track income and outflow and having a clear and detailed budget can help you to make those decisions. Tracking and budgeting give you finite numbers. Having this information helps relieve the stress. If you know what's going to happen, eliminating the stressful nature of guesswork makes a lot of difference. You'll know how much money you have to make so that you can decide whether or not to take on those clients or how many of those kinds of clients you can take on without interrupting your cash flow.

Milestones

In Chapter 9, I talked about setting goals. I recommend setting monthly, quarterly and annual financial milestones or goals.

Stop and ask, "Okay, what does it look like and is this working for me? Is this flow working? Is the revenue that's coming in actually what I projected it to be? Are the expenses remaining at the same level I thought they were going to be?"

You need to do this monthly, quarterly, and annually. Your budgets and your goals should be reviewed on that regular basis.

When you're doing this review, you're going to compare your actual finances to the budget that you set. It's going to be able to help you answer those questions if your flow is not as good as you would like it to be. What do you need to do? You need to find a remedy. What can you change? For instance, can you lessen your entertainment budget this month? Can you turn off the cable a couple of months so you can get caught back up?

What remedy do you need to find to get your budget back on track if your revenue is low or if your expenses are not quite what you thought they would be?

For instance, your landlord decides to raise the rent, or you decided to budget $1,000 for advertising and it turns out that spending $200 got you a good number of clients. Now you have an extra $800. Yes, it does happen. We find extra money sometimes too. Where can we put it to help us reach the goals that we're hoping to attain? Where can the revisions be made? Which sections in the income and the expenses can be modified?

Ask yourself what is the cause of the adjustment needed.

- What caused it to go this way?

- Do you need to permanently adjust or is it a temporary adjustment that's needed?
- What kind of adjustment needs to take place and where does it need to go into your overall plan?

Your financial goals need to include where you see yourself in your business in 3 months, 6 months, and a year. What's it going to take to get there? How much income do you need and from what sources, including what percentages and the amount of them? How many sales do you have to make to earn that amount per month, per week and per day?

To highlight the importance of careful scrutiny, I know that I wouldn't have spent thousands of dollars on educational programs if I'd had a budget that would have told me how many dollars I could spend that month. That's really an important concept.

It is amazing when you discover what you've been spending your money on and what you can get away with spending your money on. It's also very empowering because if the Yellow Page's guy calls and says, "Place an ad," and he's attempting to pressure you, you can say "I apologize, but my budget for my advertising this month has already been spent. I can no longer put any more money into it."

Put it off on your budget. Put it off on your accountant. Your accountant set you with a budget, this is all you have, and it's spent. "Thank you very much and have a nice day. Stop bothering me."

Milestones and budgets also help you with coworkers, colleagues, and sometimes even the spouse. "We've got all these bills due next week and this is the money that's coming in next week. We can't go to Disneyland or to the prime steakhouse tonight because this is what we have." It makes answering all those kinds of questions easier for you. It saves you money in the long run.

Finding a goal and knowing where you want to go is half the battle. As you grow in your business, as you grow as a person, you're going to want to change your goals: your financial goals, your business goals and your personal goals because as we change, we want changes also. I do encourage you to take some time on a regular basis either monthly or quarterly and review your goals and figure out where you want to go.

Owning a business is both challenging and rewarding. Entrepreneurship is fulfilling and encourages you to grow. Starting a business takes knowledge, persistence and courage. It is well worth the effort. Go for it!

Consider Writing a Review

Thank you for buying this book. When you enjoy a book, it is a natural desire to tell others about it. Amazon.com provides a way to share your thoughts and I invite you to write a book review. It is easy. Here are tips:

1. After going to the link below on Amazon.com, the first thing you are asked to do is to assign a number of stars to the book you think matches your opinion of the book.

2. Create a title for the review. This can be a simple phrase, like "Awesome guide." If you are not sure what to say, look at the titles of other book reviews.

3. It is easiest to write the book in a word processor and then paste it into Amazon.com. Your word processor will pick up typos before your review goes public.

4. Write the review as if you were talking to another person — you are — a person who comes to Amazon.com and is considering buying this book.

5. Include a description of what you found most helpful. Was it an idea, chapter, tip? Share that with the readers.

6. Next you may want to write who you think would most benefit from this book. Is it for beginners? Or is it more appropriate for someone with experience with this topic?

7. What if you have something negative to say about the book? You may always reach me at patiyer@legal-nursebusiness.com to suggest changes in the book.

8. If you include negative feedback in the review, keep a positive perspective rather than attack the author.

Here are some sample phrases:

- While overall the book was good, I would change it by. . .
- I don't think this book is right for. . .
- I would improve this book by. . .

Before you hit save, read everything over one more time.

Authors and readers appreciate book reviews and they get easier to write with time. Go to this link on Amazon.com to write your review. If for any reason it does not work, search for the book title + Iyer and it will show.

Link: **http://amzn.to/1MXJNQw**

Thank you,

Pat Iyer

Goodwill

Carver City Bookstores #5589
(010)517-5165
4101 SEPULVEDA BLVD, CULVER CITY, 90230
****
Store # : 1
13:35:42 1/02/18/09 52089
Computers 5   Cashier 18 :

Tot Qty   Reg Price   Sub Tot
R21303B   3.99   0   7.98
  CHAIR
R10009JR   2.99   0   5.98
  PICTURE FRAMES
B610KR13B   1.99   0   15.92
  SOFTCOVER BOOKS
B820KR19Z   2.99   0   8.97
  SOFTCOVER BOOKS

Subtotal   38.85
Total   38.85

38.85   VISA

No Exchange or Returns

Join us on Facebook and Twitter
www.goodwillsocal.org
Shop thousands of little new and treasures
by visiting our online store
www.goodwillsocal.org/donate/stores

Cashier Copy 1/02/18/09-d13:42 52089

520818852

Goodwill

Culver City Bookstore #5298
(310)574-5182
4101 SEPULVEDA BLVD, CULVER CITY 90230
****

Station # : 1
68025   03/31/2017   13:35:42

Cashier is : Cornitha S

Qty	Reg.Price		Sub.Tot
2 51303R	3.99	0	7.98
CHAIR			
1 60001R	5.99	0	5.99
PICTURE FRAMES			
6 614R0199	1.99	0	11.94
SOFTCOVER BOOKS			
2 614R0299	2.99	0	5.98
SOFTCOVER BOOKS			

Subtotal   31.89
Total   31.89

VISA   31.89

No Exchanges or Returns

Join us on Facebook and Twitter
www.Goodwillsocal.org

Shop thousands of titles and treasures
from the comfort of home 24/7
by visiting us online at
www.GoodwillSoCal.org/shop/online-store

Coupon Valid On/After 04/01/2017

5298168025

Made in the USA
San Bernardino, CA
28 June 2016